John Chalmers

Letters from the Indian Mutiny
1857 – 1859

John Chalmers
Letters from the Indian Mutiny
1857 – 1859

Presented and edited by
RICHARD TERRELL

MICHAEL RUSSELL

Editorial matter © Richard Terrell 1992

First published in Great Britain 1992
by Michael Russell (Publishing) Ltd
Wilby Hall, Wilby, Norwich

Typeset in Sabon by The Spartan Press Ltd
Lymington, Hampshire
Printed and bound in Great Britain
by Biddles Ltd, Guildford and King's Lynn

All rights reserved
ISBN 0 85955 179 2

Contents

Acknowledgements	7
Preface	9
Background to the Mutiny	13
The Events	50
Delhi	61
Lucknow	66
Jhansi	72
Cawnpore	78
John Chalmers: 1821–1859	86
The Letters	99
John Chalmers	174
Consequences	181
Index	189

A genealogical table is included
on pp. 88–9, and a map on pp. 96–7

Acknowledgements

In the Preface I have indicated the major role of Mr J. H. M. Mackenzie in the production of this book.

Acknowledgements in other books of mine share a common feature. In each I have expressed gratitude to individuals much better equipped than myself with residential opportunities for a certain kind of solitude. It is paradoxical that I should largely lack something so indispensable for the production of books, as though a gardener should possess no spade or a dentist no forceps.

I must again thank the Hon. Mrs Diana Uhlman, this time for letting me use a little room beneath the rooftops of Croft Castle in Herefordshire, overlooking a deer park and the mountains of Wales, for the incongruous purpose of describing the sieges of Delhi and Lucknow long ago. And then, in April 1990 Mr and Mrs Mackenzie kindly let me look after myself at Shellwood Manor in Surrey, in a self-contained apartment there, during a week of silent isolation when I was able to go through the initial typescript of this book.

I am grateful to Mr D. M. Spawforth, Headmaster of Merchiston Castle School at Edinburgh, for sending me a copy of an article about John Chalmers, a former pupil, written by one of his cousins for *The Merchistonian* in 1885, after John's death in Devon in the previous year.

I wish to thank the staffs of the Reading Room of the British Library, the India Office Library and Records, the Central Library in Westminster, the General Register Office for Scotland and the Public Record Office at Kew, for their patience and kindness in enabling me to trace the identities and movements of individuals, the facts of battles, the reports of parliamentary debates and the meanings of medals.

I am especially indebted to Mr Michael Anderson, of the Department of Law in the School of Oriental and African

Studies in the Universities of London, for his assistance in helping me to follow the history of the law in India about the burning of widows (suttee) from the early nineteenth century down to the present day.

Mr Christopher Hibbert and The Viking Press have kindly permitted me to quote from *The Great Mutiny*. Osprey Publishing and George Philip Ltd have kindly permitted me to reproduce the two pictures of sepoys of Native Infantry regiments of the Bengal Army, one of them loyal to the Company and the other dressed as a typical mutineer. My thanks are also due to Mr R. G. Harris, of Southsea, for drawing my attention to the original engraving of the three Sikh soldiers in uniforms presumably similar to those worn by the 24th Punjab Infantry with whom John Chalmers was associated, to Emily Wood for her reproduction of it in the correct colours, and to the National Army Museum for making a photo copy of the original available to me.

The book has been sponsored by the J. H. M. Mackenzie Charitable Trust, and I am profoundly grateful for their generous assistance.

R.T.

Preface

A Scottish friend, Mr J. H. M. Mackenzie, aware of my own interest in India, asked if I would like to see an old book, published in 1904, containing some letters from an ancestor of his, John Chalmers, written in India during the Mutiny of 1857–8. The appearance of this book is a consequence of that invitation.

The letters were published by T. & A. Constable, of Edinburgh, which no longer exists. About the turn of the present century they were discovered in a box at a house in Wishaw, a few miles from Glasgow, which had been the home of John Chalmers's mother and other members of his family. They were published privately in a small edition to commemorate the writer who had died in Devonshire in 1884.

I told Jock Mackenzie that I thought the letters ought now to be re-published, for historical reasons. Whilst John Chalmers was not a major contributor to the events of his epoch, his letters are instructive. The relatives who produced the book of 1904 were thinking of the self-portrait which they contain, that of a young man with a strong, dominant personality, great physical stamina, obvious powers of leadership and physical courage in battle, a man of whose memory they were justly proud. Today, nearly a century later, the self-portrait has become of less interest than the wider portrayal of a generation of our countrymen which the letters incidentally convey. Our understanding of the period turns essentially upon our recognition of that portrayal.

During the half century before the edition of 1904 was published, many books about the Mutiny had appeared. Few of the readers for whom the book was intended were unaware of its importance or its main incidents. Few had not seen stories of survivors and refugees. Schoolchildren knew something about the massacre at Cawnpore, the sieges of Delhi and Lucknow and the romantic figure of the Rani of Jhansi. India then was a vast, enduring feature of the world about our national life, as permanent, it seemed, as the ocean about our shores. Today, so far as the general reading public is concerned, the Indian Mutiny is now virtually lost in oblivion. In India itself there remains scanty public knowledge of the facts. In the world generally the subject is virtually confined to departments of South Asian history in various universities.

The edition of 1904 is preceded by a biographical sketch written by Isabel Grace Chalmers, a member of the family whose identity seemed at first to be in doubt. It is virtually certain, however, that her true name was Isabella Grace Pratt Chalmers. She was the youngest child of Charles Chalmers, a younger brother of John's father Patrick, and his cousin. Charles was the founder of Merchiston Castle School at Edinburgh, at which John was a pupil. She was born in 1838, seventeen years after John (born in 1821), and would have remembered him at the time when she was writing the biographical sketch at about the turn of the twentieth century. As the genealogical tree shows, Isabella was the name of her mother and Grace Pratt the names of her aunt, the wife of her father's famous elder brother, The Revd Dr Thomas Chalmers, founder of the Free Church of Scotland in 1843. The name of Pratt was used as a Christian name for two other women of the same generation of kinsfolk. It is clear from the major biography of Dr Thomas Chalmers that his wife, the original Grace Pratt, was a widely respected figure.

Whilst it seems clear that Isabel had had no personal experience of India, she may have decided that the main facts about the Mutiny were sufficiently well known to members of her own circle, for whom the book, privately printed, was intended, for anything more than a brief reference to it to seem superfluous. In this edition I have tried to do for a modern and very different readership what Isabel was unable or unwilling to do, namely to make the letters meaningful by explaining the Mutiny, its main events and its consequences for Indo-British history in the present century. I have quoted from her sketch certain passages of special interest, for reasons that will appear, but omitted most of her biographical sketch because the details it contains were of interest to a small number of relations only, and they have long been dead. The original book contains a few letters about an event after the Mutiny was over, namely, a sharp campaign against Waziri tribesmen in the hill country between the North West Frontier of India and Afghanistan. I have omitted them because the historical background is distinct from the Mutiny, and to deal with it adequately would introduce an additional and complex subject beyond my scope.

I have included some genealogical detail omitted by Isabel Grace Chalmers, and shown the links between John Chalmers and Jock Mackenzie of the present day. I am grateful to him for assistance with this.

Background to the Mutiny

By the beginning of the nineteenth century the British East India Company had become by far the most powerful military and administrative authority in the Indian subcontinent. Its ascendancy had not been the outcome of a consistent and enduring policy of imperial conquest, as is commonly assumed. It had developed over about two hundred years since the establishment of the Company on the last day of the year 1600 (with a capital of just £50,000). Long periods of consolidation had been followed by forward moves, the shifting policies of the Company and of the British government in London responding to changes in world events and to events in India itself. During the eighteenth century and early nineteenth the armed forces of the Company never included more than a small minority of British European troops. Most of the troops consisted either of those of Indian princes in alliance with the Company and the British Crown, or of Indians directly engaged as volunteers. The forces opposed to them were of a similar kind, either allied with the Crown of France, through the French East India Company, or recruited and trained by the French. Those who focus their historical telescopes upon incidents and campaigns in the conquest of India cannot, unfortunately, see with the same lenses the wider conflicts of the Seven Years War (1756–63) or the Napoleonic Wars (1797–1815), of which events in India were integral parts. Whilst British officers and soldiers in India were naturally alive to the wider context of world war, few Indians, or Indian soldiers (apart from princes themselves), were able to share that awareness. And yet, had it not been for the rivalry of Britain and France, the authority of the British East India Company, and of all British military and naval forces in the subcontinent, would probably have remained quite small and confined to trading areas near Calcutta, Bombay and Madras.

Within India itself perhaps the most important factor was the condition of the Moghul Empire, ostensibly the dominant indigenous power during the eighteenth century. It was in a phase of chronic decline, under attack from the Mahratta chiefs based upon Poona in the Western Ghats. In such conditions the Moghul power was unable to control breakaway movements by its own feudal tributary princes, maharajas and nawabs determined to set themselves up as independent powers. In the circumstances, both the French and the British companies, interested primarily in profitable trade, came into conflict with each other by seeking alliances with Indian feudal rulers, offering them military protection and financial benefits in exchange for monopolistic trading rights. The result was a complex pattern of authority, sometimes of little more than a diplomatic nature, at other times and in other parts of the country amounting to full governmental powers, military, fiscal, judicial and administrative.

In the above paragraphs I have said nothing about the constitutional relationships between the British government in London and the East India Company. Those relationships were both complex and shifting. For the purpose of this book I need go back no further than the year 1784. During the previous two decades there had been widespread concern about the Company's political and financial conduct in India, and especially about the newly acquired wealth of some of the Company's merchants who returned to Britain as conspicuous upstarts, 'nabobs' as they were called, displaying wealth whose acquisition must be dubious and whose manners were vulgar in an age of elegant grace. Such concern found its expression in the India Act of that year, on the initiative of William Pitt, the Prime Minister who succeeded Lord North after the American war. A Board of Control consisting of six privy councillors, under a president, was set up by government, the president becoming, in effect, a minister with responsibility for British policy in India. However, the new arrangement did not, in practice, imply such a strong centralization as the Act seemed to indicate. The Court of Directors in the City continued to control by patronage most of the appointments to the Company's services in India, including the military ones. And, in India itself, authority was largely split. There were three Governors at Calcutta, Bombay and Madras, each with his own appointed council of advisers, and a Governor-General (in Calcutta) with overriding authority, three armies, each with its own staff and commander-in-chief. Between 1784 and 1833 the Crown only gradually became the effective ruler of the British Indian realm, the Company becoming its managing agency, in addition to its functions as a trading concern. The constitutional structure is, and was throughout the period, complex and difficult to understand. In what follows I have virtually ignored it. For its implications were probably beyond the consciousness of John Chalmers, and entirely outside the awareness of the sepoys of the Mutiny and those of the Indian soldiers who followed him into battle against them.

In the years 1806 and 1824 there occurred in India two events which, in their essentials, closely resembled the much more widespread events of 1857–8. I shall describe them now, because the failure of the British government in London and the authorities of the Company in Calcutta to heed their warnings was probably a major cause of the great upheaval with which this book is concerned.

The first incident occurred at Vellore, about a hundred miles west-south-west of Madras. For many years its fortress had been used by the Company as a depot for troops and as a storehouse for military supplies. At various times in the previous half century it had served such purposes in complex military operations in Southern India. In that part of the country, stretching right across the peninsula to the west coast and far down to the tip of it, dominant Muslim dynasties held sway over the mass of their subjects, who were Hindus. Along the east coast, from about two hundred miles north of Madras to the southern tip of India, was the Carnatic, ruled erratically by Mohammed Ali. Another coastal strip, from the Carnatic almost as far as Puri in Orissa, was called the Northern Circars. A south-central territory was that of Mysore, over which a self-made military leader, Haidar Ali, who came originally from the Punjab, held power. By skilled military and diplomatic moves he had substantially extended the frontiers of his dominion. He had died in 1782 and been succeeded by his son Tippu Sahib, also a very considerable military leader. To the north was the large territory of the Muslim Nizam of Hyderabad, and to the west the shifting frontiers of the Hindu Peshwas of Poona, great cavalrymen, whose depredations were made at the expense of the Moghul power and all the above-mentioned Muslim rulers. The mutual relations between all these regimes, and their relations with the Company, were constantly shifting, the most disturbing factor being the almost incessant warfare between Britain and France. Haidar Ali and Tippu both secured the help of France, especially in the form of French officers and troops, in the training of their own sepoy forces for war, both against other powers in alliance with the Company, and against the Company's own British and Indian troops. The events were very complex indeed.

Tippu was killed in the course of a battle for the capital city of his dominion, Seringapatam, by the mixed Indian and British forces of Arthur Wellesley (later the Duke of Wellington), in 1799. After his defeat, the territory of Mysore was reduced to its dimensions before the time of Haidar Ali and placed under a Hindu rajah (a child at the time). The rest of it was divided between the Company and the Nizam of Hyderabad. The sons of Tippu, with their wives and families, were allowed to live on generous allowances provided by the Company, at Vellore.

In 1806, at Vellore, there was a garrison of 1,500 sepoys and 370 British troops. At 3 a.m. on 6 May a large number of the sepoys suddenly attacked the barracks of the British troops, killing about a hundred of them as they lay. About a dozen of the British officers were shot as they went out to see what was happening. The news reached Arcot, a military base sixteen miles away, at about dawn. Within a few minutes Colonel Gillespie took a squadron of cavalry from the British 19th Dragoons straight to Vellore, followed by a contingent of horse artillery. With great speed the gate of the fortress was blasted in by gunfire and the place was assaulted. About 400 of the mutineers were killed in the fighting. Many who escaped were later recaptured and promptly executed.

What caused this affair? The immediate cause was an action by a newly arrived commander-in-chief at Madras, Sir John Cradock. Unacquainted with India, he at once issued new regulations about the dress and appearance of the sepoy troops. The turbans with which they were familiar were to be abolished and replaced by a form of headgear resembling a hat. The men were not to wear earrings on parade, and were to trim their moustaches in a particular, uniform manner. These changes were interpreted by the mutineers as proof that the English intended forcibly to convert them all to Christianity. The new headgear resembled the hats worn by Indians who had been so converted.

The mutiny did not occur at once. The new regulations had been tested at Vellore on a veteran company of sepoys. They protested at them with dignity, but the commander-in-chief insisted that they should be obeyed. After some disorder nineteen men were arrested and sent to Madras for trial by court martial. Two of them were sentenced to 900 lashes and the rest to 500. The sentences were carried out on the first two, but the rest were pardoned after expressing their contrition.

After widespread objections to the regulations Cradock offered to withdraw them. But Bentinck, like Cradock, was then a very young Governor with little experience of India, and he, with the agreement of his Council, decided that the regulations must be enforced, to avoid a show of weakness. It was this insistence which caused the mutiny.

At Hyderabad, capital city of the Nizam, there was a much larger garrison of 10,000 troops, most of them sepoys, with several British units. The sepoys there, as at Vellore, protested at the regulations. The commanding officer, supported by the British resident, at once withdrew them, and there was no mutiny at Hyderabad.

The first act of the mutineers at Vellore, after killing the British troops and officers, had been to hoist the flag of the elder son of Tippu and declare that he was the new Sultan of

Mysore. All the sons of Tippu, however, and their families, were taken away by the British to Calcutta, for safe keeping, and kept there.

Lord William Bentinck went back to India in 1833 as Governor-General and soon much distinguished himself by making the burning of widows (suttee) a capital offence, and dealing with the thugs in a similar manner. The thugs went about the country for the purpose of robbing and murdering their victims, often travellers. Their activities were regarded as holy, in common with various other ritualistic gestures, including suttee itself. He abolished the flogging of Indian troops for disciplinary offences. British troops, however, continued to be flogged (almost to death) for another thirty years. Britain has always been a brutal and deeply religious country, oddly like India itself.

The second incident took place in 1824 at Barrackpore, in Bengal, quite close to Calcutta. The first Burma war (1824–26) had just started. Burma then was beyond the authority of the Company's administration. Isolated from the rest of the world by forested mountains virtually impassable during the monsoon months, its rulers and people were quite distinct from those of India, and a form of Buddhism had been the basis of their civilization for centuries.

The ruler of most of the territory was Phagyee-Dau, who had come to power in 1819 after the death of his grandfather Hpo-Dau-Hpayah. Whilst the capital city of the dynasty had for long been at Ava, near Mandalay, on the opposite side of the Irrawaddy river, Hpo-Dau-Hpayah, reputedly a tyrant, had suppressed a conspiracy to overthrow him at Ava, which he had totally destroyed. He had then moved his capital to another place, Amarapoora, no great distance away. Phagee-Dau, however, rebuilt the old capital at Ava, mainly for topographical and climatic reasons.

During previous decades the rulers at Ava had greatly expanded their territory by defeating the Arakanese and Nagas to the west and north and the Shan chiefs to the east. In war the Burmese had acquired a reputation for ferocity and military skill, neither of which attributes are commonly associated with the placid image of the Buddha. The paradox resembles that between the ferocity of Christians in their wars and the gentle image of their divinity. Anyway, the isolation of the Burmese rulers from the rest of the world had engendered a conviction that they could defeat any conceivable enemies including, they hoped, the British forces in India.

After the Burmese conquest of the various hill tribes of the West and North, great stretches of Assam and Bengal had been flooded with refugees seeking the protection of the British authority.

The British declared war against Burma on 5 March 1824 after Phagee-Dau had made aggressive movements on the territory of Chittagong, demanding that the town, together with Dacca and other centres, should be ceded to themselves and that all the refugees should be sent back to Burma. Such was the setting for the incident at Barrackpore, where a small army was being assembled to march round the coast to Chittagong, from which they were to advance into the Arakan hill tracks.

The sepoys had reasons for grievances which they discussed during the months of waiting till the passing of the monsoon in the autumn, after which the dry season would permit the advance. Each man possessed a heavy load of baggage which included, apart from his weapons and ammunition, his personal cooking and drinking vessels, a blanket and light mattress. On the march it was customary for such personal gear to be carried on the backs of bullocks whose services, plus that of a driver, had to be paid for by the sepoy out of his pay plus certain field allowances. At the time there was a considerable shortage of bullocks, which accordingly raised their cost. The shortage was acute enough to start a rumour that the British had decided to compel the troops to travel to Rangoon by sea, instead of marching overland. Finally, the morale of the sepoys was lowered by stories of the brutality of the Burmese, who were reported to mutilate or torture their prisoners, and certainly to mutilate the dead. They had already inflicted a severe reverse upon British and sepoy units at Ramu, not far away on the Arakan coast.

In the past sepoys both of Madras and Bengal had shown no objections to travel by sea. This, however, made it impossible for some of the rules of caste to be observed. On a wooden ship it was not possible for hundreds of separate meals to be cooked for men of different castes, so that common messing was unavoidable. The troops had been prepared to waive caste rules under special dispensations from their own religious authorities. However, not long before, Madras troops had travelled to Manila in the Philippines during the wars against Spain and suffered greatly in storms, many having been lost. Large bodies of sepoys had been kept away from their villages for years at a stretch by long delays caused by events at sea.

The local Indian troops intended for the campaign were the 26th, the 47th, and the 62nd Regiments of the Bengal Native Infantry. Before the end of October parties from the 26th and the 62nd had already set off towards Chittagong, taking with them the best bullocks and drivers available. The 47th were due to march on the 31st.

In the incidents of that and the following day two British officers played key roles. Colonel Cartwright, a career soldier of the Bengal Army, was in command of the 47th. He knew his men and strongly sympathized with their complaints. He had offered to meet the cost of the necessary bullocks and drivers required for his regiment entirely from his own pocket, but it is not clear whether or not this quixotic gesture was known to the men. The government had responded tardily and apparently in a niggardly way by offering to pay for ten bullocks and the necessary drivers for each company of troops, the money, however, to be advanced to the men and later deducted from their pay. Sufficient bullocks for the purpose were accordingly allotted.

Philip Mason, in *A Matter of Honour* (pp. 244–5), describes the situation on the 31st as follows:

But by this time the regiment was beyond reason. They refused to bring their knapsacks on parade, saying that they were old and unserviceable ... They said they would not go to Burma without double batta [field allowances] and would not set foot in a boat at any point on the route. Next day they refused to parade, seized the colours of the 26th regiment and threatened violence to the Brigade Commander and the Brigade Major. Finally they told Cartwright they would march only if the Government would provide the bullocks free and give them double batta, but added a new condition, that the Subadar-Major and Havildar-Major should be put to death. The Subadar-Major was a Muslim and it was alleged that he was a bully, that he had too much influence with the Colonel, and that he had threatened the Hindus that he would force them all to go in a ship. The men were eventually brought to the parade-ground, but again refused to obey Cartwright's orders. They stayed on the parade-ground the whole of November 1st – the day when they should have marched – and all night too.

The other British officer was General Sir Edward Paget who, only two years before, in 1822, had been appointed commander-in-chief of all troops, British and Indian, in the subcontinent. His career, very distinguished indeed, had been in the Netherlands, the West Indies, the Mediterranean and Spain. During the Napoleonic Wars he had been wounded in the Netherlands and lost his right arm in Spain. He had been decorated for his leadership at Coruña and been strongly commended by Wellington himself. He had had no direct experience with Indian troops.

The narrative continues:

At midnight the Commander-in-Chief, Sir Edward Paget arrived. He had ordered to Barrackpore two battalions of British infantry, a company of artillery, a troop of the Governor-General's bodyguard and the 68th Native Infantry. This imposing force arrived early on the morning of November 2nd and was immediately drawn up on the parade-ground covering the 47th, who presented the Commander-in-Chief with a petition. This repeated their fears of being sent by sea; they begged to be discharged in a body and allowed to go home. Sir Edward Paget replied that he understood their objection to going by sea, that he had never ordered any sepoy to go by ship unless he agreed and would listen to them further, but that they must first lay down their arms and surrender unconditionally. But they refused to ground arms and a party seized and destroyed the colours of the 26th, ... At this Paget ordered two guns to open fire on the 47th. They were loaded with case or canister. The mutineers broke and fled; they offered no resistance. Indeed, their muskets were not loaded. Few were killed but many wounded; a number were taken prisoner. That day, November 2nd, a native court martial sentenced 41 prisoners to death. Of these twelve were executed next day; the sentences on the others were commuted to hard labour. The regiment was disbanded and the number erased from the Army List.

Having dealt with the mutiny at Barrackpore, Paget at once turned his attention to the main job in hand, the conduct of the war. Considerable success was achieved in the South by the capture of Rangoon and much of the southern coastal region. The jungled hills of the West and North, however, presented enormous obstacles. Peace was concluded in 1826, the Burmese ceding much of the Arakan and the hilly regions to the north, together with a long strip of coastal territory along the Bay of Bengal.

My reasons for describing the incidents at Vellore and Barrackpore are presentational. For both were characteristic of virtually all the major incidents which ensued on a much bigger scale a few decades later. If, therefore, the reader has in his mind a general idea of them in advance, an attempt to discover a few overriding causes of the major tragedy lying ahead may be illuminated for him. That is what I hope. How did it come about that the warnings of Vellore and Barrackpore were insufficiently heeded? Many writers on the Mutiny have lamented the failure and most have contented themselves by listing the proximate causes of each event to come. Can we go deeper?

In 1793 the Charter of the East India Company had been extended for another twenty years. In 1812 and 1813, therefore the British government had to decide whether or not the Charter should be extended for a further period, and if so how long and on what terms? The whole future of Indo-British relations must turn upon those decisions.

The debates in Parliament reveal most vividly the concern of responsible people in Britain about the gravity of the discussions and the difficulties of arriving at decisions about the future of the Company. In what follows I have quoted at some length from some of the most important speeches. For many months, both in the Lords and the Commons discussions about proposals for amending the terms of the Charter were held almost every week. The debates in the old, unreformed Parliament, twenty years before the Reform Bill of 1832, were of astonishing eloquence and great integrity.

The Napoleonic War had been almost continuous for about twenty years and the Battle of Waterloo still lay ahead. The global military situation is easy to forget today as one sits in a library reading on microfilm the parliamentary debates of 1813. One is reminded of it suddenly by the occasional interruptions of the proceedings, arranged at short notice, to enable the Lords and Commons to send messages of thanks to the Duke of Wellington for his victories in Spain: Cuidad Rodrigo (January 1812); Badajoz (April 1812) Vittoria (June 1813) and Salamanca (July 1813).

The impact of the war, and of the earlier wars of the age, upon the debates about the future of the Company was twofold. First, Napoleon's mastery of Europe had enabled him to impose a blockade of British trade with the Continent. This had caused much distress and unemployment in British ports and industrial centres. Ever since its establishment at the beginning of the seventeenth century, the East India Company had enjoyed a complete statutory monopoly of the trade between those parts of the subcontinent under Company control and Britain, and all the merchandise of the company destined for Britain had to be shipped to London, other ports being excluded from the trade. This monopolistic feature of the Charter was now under attack. In 1812 petitions from interested parties in many parts of the country were laid before Parliament by members, on behalf of their constituents. All of them requested that the Charter, if extended, should be amended to permit independent traders to go to India to compete with the Company on its own ground, and that other British ports should be thrown open to the India trade.

The second impact was of a psychological nature, generated by British victories during the current war. It was reinforced, moreover, by the changed position of Britain during the previous century. Since 1688 Britain had risen from the position of a second-class European power to become the most powerful imperial and maritime power in the world.* Hitherto the main objectives of British people in distant parts of the world had been assumed, in responsible circles, to be broadly those of profitable trade and something vaguely indicated by the word 'adventure', however altruistic or piratical the adventure might be. The debates of 1813, however, now demonstrated that those objectives were no longer adequate for future policy, especially with regard to India. For, in the previous decades the Company's responsibilities could no longer be defined as limited to commerce, but, over vast stretches of the subcontinent, had become those of government itself. Even if the entire profitability of British trade in India were to crumble into loss, the responsibility of government would remain, unless the entire British presence in India were to be withdrawn without consideration of the future.

By 1813 the financial position of the company was actually far from secure. It was, indeed, far too complicated for most members of the House of Commons to understand anyway. Apart from the cost of much warfare in India, the Company had invested large sums in improving the capital infrastructure of the country by making roads, together with canals that were used, not only as a means of transport but as sources of water for irrigation. A large new administrative, judicial, fiscal and military public service had to be provided for on a recurrent basis. Such expenditure was beyond the taxable resources of the country, so the British government had to come to the Company's assistance. In retrospect, on financial grounds alone there seems to have been a case for terminating the Charter and withdrawing the entire British presence from India. That alternative, which would have appealed to British politicians of our own day (as it did in the years after the Second World War) would not have been popular in 1813. The mood of imperial euphoria engendered by the military situation, and by the feeling of global responsibility for everything whatever, ruled out any such negative decisions.

*This phenomenon has been the subject of a recent study – John Brewer, London, 1989.

But, if the great Indian realm was not to be abandoned, what should be done about it?

In the debates the principal contributors were members with personal experience of India, a vocal handful in an assembly of colleagues who could only listen and decide the outcome. The main exception was the great and solemn evangelical reformer, William Wilberforce himself. He admitted that he had never been to India, and went on to deliver a speech of immense length, so convincing as to dominate the House and the government entirely.

In 1813 the numerous petitions and motions were discussed in a committee of the whole House. On 30 March Warren Hastings, the former Governor-General of India, was called from retirement at the age of seventy-nine to give evidence. There was probably no man whose experience of India, extending over most of his life, gave him a stronger title to be heard. His evidence, in the form of answers to questions addressed to him by speakers on behalf of the Company, took up twelve columns of the official report. Here are a few passages:

Q. If Europeans were permitted to sojourn in India, according to their own pleasure, and without any restraint what would the effect of that be?

A. Most hurtful and most ruinous, both to the Company's interest, and to the government, and to the peace of the country . . . The native Indian is weak in body and timid in spirit; he is not susceptible of restraint, but without the feeling of shame, which, under the appellation of honour, in the breast of an European, makes resentment a species of law, and which over-rules the fear of law, pain, danger and death. This is not the absolute character of the people taken in the mass; the native Indian is individually such as I have described him; but there are cases in which a provocation of general grievance would excite a whole people, and even a detached number of them, to all the ferocities of insurrection . . . The Englishman is quite a different character in India; the name of an Englishman is both his protection, and a sanction for offences he would not dare to commit at home . . . The aggrieved Indian has no chance with such a disparity; he may apply to the nearest provincial court of justice, but the difficulties, which could hardly be apprehended in any other country, arrest and impede him: the distance often from the magistrate requiring more time than he can spare; the expenses and delays of the established courts would be an impediment to any Indian to have recourse to it: the difficulty of obtaining the attendance of witnesses, would be very great and almost insurmountable, from the same cause, and, added to the other causes, would be more likely to prevent his complaining at all, than to quicken a sense of injury to induce him to complain on slight occasions; besides, the affinity of national appellations, language, manners, dress, and possibility of social intercourse between his oppressor and his judge, would impress him with an awe, which the other would either not feel or feel in a very small degree. Such I know would be the effect of a single European, not dependent upon the Company's service, residing at a distance from the seat of government, among the natives of India. But if it is proposed to let loose hordes of men of that character, I think the consequence can be no less than ruin to the peace of the country and to the interests of the Company.

Q. Do you consider that this unrestrained liberty of Europeans sojourning in India, would lead generally to acts of tyranny and oppression upon the natives, by the Europeans or Englishmen so sojourning at liberty?

A. It certainly would.

Q. Do you conceive it to be possible practically to restrain Europeans sojourning in India according to their own pleasure, to such a residence at the principal settlements or seats of government, as would counteract the effects which you apprehend from such sojournment?

A. I think it not practicable. This was not always my opinion: I did think that Europeans not in the Company's service, might be confined to the principal settlements, or to certain boundaries without them, by certain well-defined and unqualified restrictions; and that with such a guard, the admission of free traders into the country would not only be innoxuous but even beneficial ... But if a law should be enacted, against the sense and remonstrance of the Company, empowering British adventurers without distinction to go to India, but confining them to the principal settlements, I think they would transgress the bounds of that law ...

Q. Is not the character of the native Indian in its nature stationary and immutable, and not apt to vary from the original habits of the country?

A. It certainly is very stationary, I do not know whether it can be pronounced immutable; any constitutional alteration in the system of polity and jurisprudence, as it may afford an opening to new hopes or excite new fears, may give a new direction to their tempers; still the Hindoo would remain materially the same: the general conformation of their bodies, on which the physical and moral character of man depends, is not likely to undergo any alteration: in effect I believe that the Indians now are in their dress, their manners, and in all the habits of life, just what they were at the commencement of the period of their present juge or age, which is perhaps as far as the history of that country extends.

Q. What in your opinion would be the consequences, if persons were to be allowed to employ themselves as missionaries in converting the natives to the Christian religion, unlicenced and subject to no restraint on the part of the Company?

A. ... I cannot tell what the effect would be generally; if such a case had happened when I held the first place in the government of India, and such persons demeaned themselves properly, I should have taken no notice of them; but if they gave occasion to a belief that the government itself tacitly encouraged their designs, from no apparent apprehension of the consequences which such a belief would produce upon the minds of the people, and especially the irritable spirits of the Mahomedans, I certainly should have checked the attempt, and withdrawn them to Calcutta, or, if they afforded sufficient cause for it, compelled them to quit the country; when I speak of myself in the first person, I mean I should have recommended that conduct to the members of the government over which I presided.

Q. What is your opinion as to the political effect of the measure proposed, respecting a church establishment for India?

A. *The question is one of great intricacy, and of such delicacy, that I should almost fear to speak of it . . . May I say without offence, that I wish any other time had been chosen for it? A surmise has gone forth, of an intention of this govenment to force our religion upon the consciences of the people of India, who are subject to the authority of the Company; it has pervaded every one of the three establishments of Bengal, Fort St George and Bombay, and has unhappily impressed itself with peculiar force upon the minds of our native infantry, the men upon whom we must depend in the last resort for our protection against any disturbances which might be the effect of such surmises. Much would depend upon the temper, conduct, and demeanour of the person elevated to that sacred office. I dare not say all that is in my mind upon this subject, but it is one of great hazard.*[My italics.]

The above extracts form a small part of the examination of the great Warren Hastings in his old age. Those I have quoted were selected, rather than any others, because they constitute the clearest forebodings of what was to come a few decades later.

Apart from Warren Hastings, the two most prominent speakers with personal experience of India were the father and son, Charles Grant, Senior and Junior. The elder man spoke with greater authority but his eloquence did not compare with that of his son. The son's contribution earned him considerable fame and is a joy to read, both for its style and profundity. For those reasons I have quoted from it at length. I have not quoted from the various speeches of Charles Grant, Senior, whose career, however, put him in a very strong position indeed.

Charles Grant, Senior was born in 1746 in Inverness. He went to India in 1767 as a young army officer to the service of the Company in Bengal. On his arrival he was at once posted to the civil service through the patronage of a member of the Bengal Council. He returned to Scotland in 1770 where, in Inverness, he married Jane Fraser, and returned to India as a writer on the Bengal establishment in 1772. Thereafter he had an outstanding career in the mercantile and administrative service of the Company. In 1773 he became a factor and secretary to the Board of Trade in Calcutta. In 1781 he was promoted to be commercial resident in charge of the silk factory at Malda, about 150 miles north of Calcutta, near the Ganges. He became a senior merchant in 1884 and soon made a large fortune in lucrative trade. Cornwallis, the Governor-General, gave him superintendence of all the Company's trade in Bengal.

In Calcutta Grant had been much influenced by the personality and zeal of the Danish missionary, Frederick Swartz. In 1792 he wrote an influential pamphlet *Observations on the State of Society among the Asiatic Subjects of Great Britain*, in which he advocated the toleration of missionary and educational work in the East. In 1802, back in Britain, Grant entered Parliament as the member for Invernesshire. In 1804 he became Deputy

Chairman of the Court of Directors of the Company and Chairman in 1805. In the debates of 1813 he opposed the anti-missionary policy of Hastings and was a strong supporter of Wilberforce. He retired from Parliament in 1818. He died in 1823.

Charles Grant, Junior was born at Kidderpore in 1778. He came to England with his family in 1790, so that only his first twelve years were spent in India. He became a distinguished Cambridge scholar, travelled widely in Europe, wrote a book about ancient mythology and was known in society as a bright intellectual commentator on current affairs. He entered Parliament in 1811 as the member for Invernesshire Fortrose Burgh in 1811. In 1812 he distinguished himself by an able maiden speech in support of a bill of Castlereagh's on the subject of law and order, and in the following year by his second, even more effective speech about the East India Company. I will summarize the rest of his career after quoting the latter speech. It was delivered on 31 May and covered over twenty columns of the report.

· Much of the first half of Grant's speech need not detain us, crucial though it was to the debate, for it concerned the past achievements of the Company and certain important problems which must face it in the future, particularly those of what was called 'patronage', comprising the appointments, transfers, promotions and the award of honours, in an epoch characterized by nepotism, political favours and corruption, whether in India or in Europe. The age of competitive examinations had not yet begun. On the main proposals before the House, namely those affecting the permission of free mercantile competition with the Company, Grant was critical of the academic doctrines of Adam Smith and the theoretical adherents of free trade. Here are extracts from the main and latter parts of his speech:

Whatever other topics of difference may prevail, there is one point in which all parties coincide; and that is in the representation of the character and habits of the Hindoos. They are a people, it is universally acknowledged, whose manners and modes of life continue to a remarkable degree the same from age to age. Their wants are few; their diet, their clothing, their cottages, or rather their huts, all are on the same scale of frugality – their climate excites no extravagant desires – their soil demands little culture, all that they require they find among themselves. Everything contributes to make them stationary: and all these tendencies are rivetted and rendered irresistible by the nature of their religion. Never was there a religion which so mixed itself with all the transactions of life, social, civil and domestic; it entwines itself with every part of daily conduct; it regulated even the lowest and most trivial actions, and regulates them, not by the invisible energy of a pervading influence, but by arbitrary and specific enactments applicable to the minutest particulars. It perpetuates the existing system of manners and prejudices, by clothing it with the sanctions of divine authority, and guards it from the effects of foreign example or persuasion. Like its own favourite emblem, the mysterious serpent, it lulls its votary to rest amongst its voluminous evils; while with fierce eye and lifted crest it forbids the approach of unhallowed intrusion. But there is mortality in the embrace of those folds, they paralyse whatever they envelope and the sleep which they protect is the sleep of death . . .

Three thousand years have rolled away, and this people are nearly in the same situation as at the commencement of that period. During that time, how many fluctuations have occurred! What revolutions have taken place! How many great nations have been swept from the face of the earth. Their own country had been repeatedly desolated by invading armies. Their oppressors have triumphed and passed away. The lordly house of Timour has risen, and flourished, and decayed. Nature herself has suffered convulsions. The mountain has sunk, – the valley has been filled, – the Ganges has changed its course, while those who drink of its waters remain the same, bound up in the same customs, involved in the same prejudices, abandoned to the same superstitions.

It is not enough to say that they have recently submitted to many alterations, that they obey our laws and serve in our armies. I do not speak of their political or national conditions, – in this respect they have undergone perpetual vicissitudes. I speak of their social and domestic manners and opinions; and the fact that in the midst of so many political changes, their domestic and personal system, civil and religious, should have continued unchanged, is itself only an additional confirmation of these general remarks: this fact, I venture to repeat, is unquestionable. The private life of the Hindoo at this moment is precisely what it was at the time of Alexander's expedition; nor could a modern traveller describe it in terms more appropriate than those employed by the pen of Arrian.

If this be true, is there any prospect of a sudden or speedy change? Or can the fiat of a British parliament at once and in a moment transform those millions into consumers of British manufactures? If any change takes place, it must be gradual, and cannot be sensibly felt till after the lapse of many years. And yet it is for the purpose of immediate relief that the distressed manufacturers of this country have been incited to clamour for a free trade with India . . .

But let it be admitted, Sir, that the wildest expectations of the most sanguine will be realised; still the great question remains; how will this affect the people of India? For this, it should never be forgotten, is the enquiry upon which our decision must turn; and I am almost ashamed to have dwelt so long on any other branch of the subject. We are legislating for India, for the happiness of India; and I ask, what will be the influence of a large and almost unlimited admission of European adventurers into that country? For let it be recollected, that this vast increase of British exports to India, this vast augmentation of commercial intercourse between the two countries, necessarily supposes an admission of Europeans into these territories far beyond the utmost number which are at present admitted. It is obvious indeed that the one could not take place without the other; and then I ask, is there no danger to the people of India? Is it reasonable to suppose that men rushing into that scene with the sole anxiety for wealth, would be always very scrupulous as to the means of attaining it? We have heard much of the honourable British trader, and certainly no man is more disposed than I am to do justice to that high character. From those distinguished men who by extending our commerce extend our prosperity and fame, and of whom it would be easy to name many both within and without these walls, I should expect not only everything that is enlarged and generous in honour and humanity. If these were the persons to whom the fortunes of India were to be trusted; if those hon. gentlemen whom I have now the honour to see in this House were themselves to be present in every vessel that sailed for the East, there might be less room for apprehension . . . But does any man believe that a majority or even a considerable part of those who would take advantage of a less restricted intercourse, would be composed of this class of merchants? Do we not know that far the greater number would be adventurers of desperate or needy circumstances, burning to try their fortunes on that distant and boundless stage, and ambitious only to enrich themselves in the shortest possible space of time, — is it likely that they should regard the welfare of the natives as their prime concern; that they should be alive to their feelings and susceptibilities? Amid so many temptations and so much impunity, would they be always awake to the claims and interests of these people? Would they never be guilty of severity, injustice and oppression? The apprehensions which I express are not chimerical; they are justified by our past experience . . .

I think that no man ought to give a vote which may tend to endanger the present system, unless he is convinced upon personal examination, that it will be replaced by a system exempt from its inconveniences, and likely to bestow at least equal benefits; and I venture to assert that such a vote unsupported by such a conviction will involve in it a dereliction of duty. In maintaining the system which has been the parent of so many blessings to India, we shall find our recompense in the gratitude of that people; and if that recompence should be denied to us, yet when we look on the moral cultivation and progressive felicity of those regions, and when we reflect that these are the fruits of our wise and disinterested policy, we shall enjoy a triumph still more glorious and elevated; a delight infinitely surpassing the golden dreams of commercial profit, or the wildest Elysium ever struck out by the ravings of distempered avarice.

Throughout his speech Grant made no explicit reference to the crucial matter of Christian missionaries and the part which should, or should not, be played by the established Church in India. The nearest he got to it was the eloquent passage in the last few lines about the 'moral cultivation and progressive felicity' of the Indian people which it should be the policy of Britain to promote. His later position, however, is evident from his career. In 1818 he succeeded his father as member for the County of Invernesshire. In 1819 he became Chief Secretary for Ireland and a member of the Privy Council. In 1830 he became President of the Board of Control of the East India Company, retaining that position till the end of 1834. In 1833 he was responsible for legislation under which the Charter of the Company was again extended, with important amendments. It ceased altogether to be a trading company, surrendering all its mercantile interests to the government in exchange for an annuity and certain financial guarantees. Bishoprics were established for Bombay and Madras. A bishopric had already been established at Calcutta in 1813, together with archdeaconries in the three main centres of India.

In 1835 Grant became Colonial Secretary, and was raised to the peerage as Lord Glenelg. He abolished the slave trade in the West Indies. He resigned from the government in 1839 over a difference of policy affecting Canada. He died in 1866, unmarried.

So far as India was concerned, the philosophy of Grant's speech of 1813 seems now to have been diametrically opposed to the policy he pursued in 1833, which had the effect of 'privatizing' the whole India trade, the Company retaining only its political, judicial, administrative and military roles. How did this affect the Mutiny to come? Much less, I think, than might have been expected in the light of the eloquence of 1813. But let us now turn to William Wilberforce.

Wilberforce (1759–1833), a member of Parliament from 1780 to 1825 representing several constituencies in succession, was very well known to all the statesmen of his day, though he was never himself a minister of the Crown. His entire career was concerned with measures of social reform, including the criminal law, the abolition of the slave trade and of slavery itself. But, so far as India was concerned, his evangelical determination to promote Christian belief throughout the planet was, I believe, the most important contributory cause of the Mutiny of 1857. I take that view because, in all the main centres of the Mutiny, the mutineers themselves acted upon the assumption that the British government was determined to impose Christianity upon them by force, at the point of the bayonet. They resisted with bayonets of their own.

In the context of this book it is of considerable interest that, in the days before Wilberforce's great speech about India on 22 June 1813, he was lobbied intensively by many of the evangelical leaders in the country, but especially by the most famous of them all, Dr Thomas Chalmers, DD, the elder brother of the father of John Chalmers. When the latter arrived in India in 1849, not as a missionary but as a corporal in the Royal Corps of Sappers and Miners, his familiarity with the figure of Wilberforce, and that of his famous uncle Thomas, must have been shared with most of his contemporaries.

Wilberforce's speech was overwhelming by its duration alone, taking up no less than thirty-one columns of the report. Whilst Charles Grant, Junior had confined himself almost exclusively to the proposed free trade in India for independent merchants, Wilberforce confined himself to the proposals about Christian missionaries. Wilberforce was a reformer, not an economist.

After admitting that he possessed no personal experience of India, he declared that he had made up for it by diligent study of the works of travellers going far back into the past and down to his own times. His long speech was intended to have two main effects: to make the hair of hon. members stand on end with horror at descriptions of customs prevalent in India from the earliest records down to his own time, and to impress upon them their moral duty to do something about it. Passive spectatorship was understandable so long as the Company was no more than a trading organization on the coastal fringes of India. Now that it had become the predominant sovereign authority over vast stretches of the country, such passivity had ceased to be either practicable or morally tolerable. No confrontation with the evil in Indian society could be successful, however, unless a great many Indians could themselves be brought to recognize the evil in their midst and join us in suppressing it. The inculcation of Christian doctrine was the only available method of creating such recognition among the people of India. However, Wilberforce was at pains to stress that he was concerned not merely with the spread of Christian moral values, but with education at all levels and the spread of useful knowledge of every kind for the enlightenment of the people of India.

At the outset he used expressions common to the evangelists of the period, including especially Dr Thomas Chalmers himself:

I grant that it is much to be regretted, and among the Roman Catholics it has been the reproach of the Protestant churches, that they have taken so little interest in the conversation of the heathen nations; and I may take this opportunity if declaring it as my opinion, that it is much to be regretted, that our excellent church establishment contains within itself no means of providing fit agents for the important work of preaching Christianity to the heathen.

And:

It is obvious, that the qualifications required in those who discharge the duties of the ministerial office in this highly civilized community, are very different from those for which we ought chiefly to look, in men whose office it will be to preach the Gospel to the heathen nations, which they will find unacquainted with the first principles of religion and morality; from the qualifications which we should require in instructors who will probably be cast among barbarians and, besides having to encounter the grossest ignorance and its attendant vice . . .

Before getting down to specific Indian horrors, he quoted the works of travellers from early times down to the present day whose accounts of Indian morality and social customs were uniformly opprobrious. Such accounts, however, were all expressed in general terms.

By enlightening the minds of the natives, we should root out their errors, without provoking their prejudices; and it would be impossible that men of enlarged and instructed minds could continue enslaved by such a monstrous system of follies and superstitions as that under the yoke of which the natives of Hindostan now groan. They would, in short, become Christians, if I may so express myself, without knowing it . . .

And now, Sir, let me enter into the discussion, by assuring the House, that there never was a subject which better deserved the attention of a British parliament than that which we are now deliberating. Immense religions, with a population amounting, as we are assured, to sixty millions of souls, have providentially come under our dominion. They are deeply sunk, and by their religious superstition fast bound, in the lowest depths of moral and social wretchedness and degradation . . .

Our opponents confidently assure us, that we may spare ourselves the pains; for that the natives of Hindostan are so firmly, nay, so unalterably, attached to their own religious opinions and practices, however unreasonable they may appear to us, that their conversion is utterly impracticable . . .

In several columns of the report, Wilberforce demonstrated

that in the past, great numbers of Indians had, in fact, changed their religious beliefs for the better, as in the case of the Buddhism of Akbar, the religion of the Sikhs and, especially in the South, that of the Christians, especially those of the Roman Catholic faith.

He went on:

... let me quote to you some general opinions of the moral state of the Hindoos, which have been given by authors of established credit, as well as by others whose authority is still higher, persons who held high stations in the Company's service for many years, and who, from having lived so long, and having had so much intercourse with them, must be supposed to have been perfectly acquainted with their real character. Several of the passages which I am about to read to you, are contained in a most valuable document lately laid before the House, the work of a dear and most honoured friend of mine, a member of this House, whose excellent understanding and acknowledged worth entitle all his opinions to be received with the utmost deference

The document was written by Charles Grant, Senior – *Observations on the State of Society among the Asiatic Subjects of Great Britain*. Other quotations included the following:

[From Orme's history of the Carnatic, published some years before:] Were not the Gentoos infamous for the want of generosity and gratitude in all the commerces of friendship; were they not a tricking, deceitful people in all their dealings ...

Every offence is capable of being expiated by largesses to the brahmins, prescribed by themselves according to their own measures of avarice and sensuality.

[Of the Mohamedans:] A domineering insolence towards all who are in subjection to them, ungovernable wilfulness, inhumanity, cruelty, murders, and assassinations, perpetuated with the same calmness and subtelty as the rest of their politics, and insensibility to remorse for these crimes, which are scarcely considered otherwise than as necessary accidents in the course of life; sensual excesses, which revolt against nature; unbounded thirst of power, and a rapaciousness of wealth equal to the extravagance of his propensities and vices!

[Quoting from Sir John Shore (Governor General 1793–8, now Lord Teignmouth:] The natives are timid and servile: individuals have little sense of honour, and the nation is wholly void of public virtue. They make not the least scruple of lying, where falsehood is attended with advantage. To lie, to steal, plunder, ravish, or murder, are not deemed sufficient crimes to merit expulsion from society.

Lord Cornwallis proved by his conduct that he considered the natives as unworthy of all confidence; for, contrary to the general usage of men occupying such stations as he filled, he never reposed any trust in any one of them, nor placed a single individual, either Hindoo or Mahomedan, about his person, above the rank of a menial servant.

A melancholy proof of the low standard of morals in the East was affordd on one of the occasions which drew from Sir James Mackintosh [an account of the following story]: A woman who was one of the witnesses, having prevaricated shockingly, was asked by the Recorder, 'Whether there was any harm in false swearing?' she answered 'that she understood the English had a great horror of it, but there was no such horror in her country'.

Sir James Mackintosh had been Recorder of Bombay in the last decade of the eighteenth century.

Many more quotations of a similar kind followed.

Halfway through his speech, Wilberforce paused to consider a proposal already before the House, namely that, instead of attempting to turn Indians into Christians, a seemingly impossible task, we should find means of propagating among them the finest moral traditions of their own religions, especially those of Hinduism and Islam, for that, surely, would be more likely to meet with success. He rejected this, however, because no such refinements of Indian religious doctrines could exclude from them certain major evils, such as caste, the subordination of women, polygamy and infanticide, all of which were practised on a gigantic scale, and had been so from very early times. No, he insisted, there was no substitute for Christianity. Caste doomed great masses of humanity to perpetual, hereditary degradation. The evils of the other religious values were manifest.

He went on to describe in graphic detail the custom of widow burning, or suttee. Quoting the evidence of certain missionaries, he said that, in a single district near Calcutta, in a small area, no less than 130 widows had been burnt in a period of six months a few years before the year 1803, but in that year, in the same space, 275, including a girl of eleven years of age, had been burnt.

I ought to state, that the utmost pains were taken to have the account correct; certain persons were employed purposely to watch and report the number of these horrible exhibitions; and the place, person, and other particulars were regularly certified. After hearing this, you will not be surprised on being told, that the whole number of these annual sacrifices of women, who are often thus cruelly torn from their children at the very time when from the loss of their father, then must have been in the greatest need of the fostering care of the surviving parent, is estimated, I think, in the Bengal provinces, to be 10,000; . . .

Nor must we dare to flatter ourselves, though it would in truth be a wretched consolation, that, as has been sometimes stated, these sacrifices are spontaneous. . . . the women are always fastened down, sometimes with strong green bamboos, at others with thick strong ropes thoroughly soaked in water; which is done, as Mr Marshman was frankly told, lest on feeling the fire they should run away and make their escape; Bernier goes on 'When the wretched victims drew back, I have seen those demons the brahmins thrusting them into the fire with their long poles'. Sometimes, indeed, the relations and friends of the widow, exerting their utmost influence with her, succeed in persuading her to live; but too commonly, the poor wretches are forced into these acts of self-immolation by the joint influence of their hopes and fears. Their fears, however, are by far the more predominant of the two: and while the brahmins delude them with the hopes of glory and immortality if they confine themselves to the flames, their only alternative is a life of hard fare, and servile offices; in sort, a life of drudgery, degradation and infamy.

In a subsequently printed version of the speech, Wilberforce included this:

It would scercely be justifiable to forbear inserting, what perhaps I was culpable in not reading to the House, the following account of one of these horrible scenes, at which the missionary Mr Marshman, was present a few years ago. I will extract his own words, only adding, that he is a man of the most established integrity . . .

A person informing us that a woman was about to be burnt with the corpse of her husband, near our house, I, with several of our brethren, hastened to the place: but before we could arrive, the pile was in flames. It was a horrible sight. The most shocking indifference and levity appeared among those who were present. I never saw anything more brutal than their behaviour. The dreadful scene had not the least appearance of a religious ceremony. It resembled an abandoned rabble of boys in England, collected for the purpose of worrying to death a cat or a dog. A bamboo, perhaps twenty feet long, had been fastened at one end to a stake driven into the ground, and held down over the fire by men at the other. Such was the confusion, the levity, the bursts of brutal laughter, while the poor woman was burning alive before their eyes, that it seemed as if every spark of humanity was extinguished by this accursed superstition. That which added to the cruelty was the smallness of the fire. It did not consist of so much as we consume in dressing a dinner: no, not this fire that was to consume the living and the dead! I saw the legs of the poor creature hanging out of the fire while her body was in flames. After a while, they took a bamboo ten or twelve feet long and stirred it, pushing and beating the half consumed corpses, as you would repair a fire of green wood, by throwing the unconsumed pieces into the middle. Perceiving the legs hanging out, they beat them with the bamboo for some time, in order to break the ligatures which fastened them at the knees (for they would not have come near to touch them for the world). At length they succeeded in bending them upwards into the fire, the skin and muscles giving way, and discovering the knee sockets bare, with the balls of the leg bones: a sight this which, I need not say, made me thrill with horror, especially when I recollected that this hapless victim of superstition was alive but a few minutes before. To have seen savage wolves thus tearing a human body, limb from limb, would have been shocking; but to see the relations and neighbours do this to one with whom they had familiarly conversed not an hour before, and to do it with an air of levity, was almost too much for me to bear.

You expect, perhaps, to hear, that this unhappy victim was the wife of some brahmin of high cast. She was the wife of a barber who dwelt in Serampore, and had died that morning, leaving the son I have mentioned, and a daughter of about eleven years of age. Thus had this infernal supertition aggravated the common miseries of life, and left these children, stripped of both their parents in one day. Nor is this an uncommon case. It often happens to children far more helpless than these; sometimes to children possessed of property, which is then left, as well as themselves, to the mercy of those who have decoyed their mother to their father's funeral pile!

In the resulting legislation the mercantile monopoly of the Company was broken, and independent traders were allowed to go to India and compete with those of the Company, subject to certain safeguards against unscrupulous conduct on their part. The monopoly of the Company's trade with China (with the export of Indian opium to China) was preserved. The evil of the opium trade, producing handsome profits, was overlooked, with tragic consequences. The position of the established Church was much strengthened by creating a bishopric in Calcutta and archdeaconries in Calcutta, Madras and Bombay. Subject to safeguards, missionaries of miscellaneous Christian sects were allowed. The introduction of missionaries was not wholly new, for a few of them, including especially Baptists, had already been active in India for many years. The debate was interpreted as having been concerned not so much with the importance of missionary work as such but the extent to which the British government and the Company should be officially pronounced as intent upon the mass conversion of 'the heathen' in India to Christianity. The act was very carefully worded to evade explicit commitment to any such objective. In short, British ministers and Parliamentarians, then as now, were at pains to discover forms of words conducive to the creation of 'elbow room' for the future.

Let us now stand back from the debate of 1813 to consider the period in retrospect. For our interpretation of it must, I believe, have a profound effect upon our understanding of the Indian Mutiny to come over forty years later.

It seems to me that, had it not been for the overwhelming ethos of imperial grandeur which obsessed the British people as a whole, a patriotic euphoria of recent growth since the revolution of 1688, the debate about the future of the East India Company would have had a different outcome. The views of the India experts, such as Warren Hastings and Charles Grant, Junior, would have prevailed. The trading monopoly of the Company would have been preserved for longer and the evangelical movement would have been much less assertive. I doubt if bishops or archdeaconries would have been set up at all. The numbers of Europeans in India would no doubt have grown considerably after the opening of the overland route in 1830, but I doubt if they would have differed greatly in their attitudes to Indians from their predecessors of the eighteenth century. The early Victorians would not have been so arrogantly Victorian as they became in fact in India. It would have been sufficient to have appreciated any Indians who, in the decades ahead, might perhaps decide to adopt customs similar to those of Europeans, without the aid of explicitly Christian mentors intent upon changing their religious beliefs.

As for suttee, thuggee and the maltreatment of children and cruelties associated with the caste system, changes in the law to deal with them on purely secular lines were initiated in 1833. In that year (following the great parliamentary reform of the previous year), two important steps affecting India were taken. First, under the Charter Act, all the remaining trading and commercial functions of the Company were abolished, leaving the Company as the sole political and administrative agency for the government of India under the Crown. Second, in order to reduce anomalous differences in judicial administration in different parts of India, and, so far as possible to eliminate discrimination in the treatment of Indian and British persons by the courts of the Company, the Indian Law Commission was appointed, under the presidency of Macaulay, for the formidable purpose of codifying the whole of the criminal and civil laws of the country. Lord William Bentinck, the Governor-General (1828–35), notwithstanding his own evangelical inclinations, supported these important moves.

The Indian Penal Code, drafted almost single-handedly by Macaulay, defined suttee as 'voluntary culpable homicide by consent', the typical case being illustrated thus: 'Z, a Hindoo widow, consents to be burned with the corpse of her husband. A kindles the pile. Here A has committed voluntary culpable homicide by consent.' The punishments for that offence were 'imprisonment . . . for a term which may extend to fourteen years, a fine or both.' The precise sentence was left to the court. The offence of thuggee was defined as murder, for which the sentence was death. For various reasons the new penal code and the new codes of criminal and civil procedure, were not actually applied till 1860–1. They were warmly welcomed by Indians generally, and are still the foundation of the legal system of India to this day.

During the parliamentary debate of 1813, even experienced contributors with long acquaintanceship with India did not appreciate the extent to which the people of India, by virtue of the enduring nature of princely rule and personal authority in their own history, associate the charisma of a ruler (whether British or any other) with the firmness of his decisions rather than the content of his policies. Macchiavelli understood this, but Britain has never been such a haven for Macchiavellian statesmen as the world is inclined to assume. It seems to me likely that, had the British government firmly announced that it had decided to convert the people of India into Christians, by force if necessary, vast numbers of Indians, including thousands of sepoys in the armies of the Company, would have hailed the announcement with applause. But to permit the influx of Christian missionaries, on the one hand, whilst disclaiming any policy of mass conversion with a gesture of the other, was not conducive to comprehension by any Indians at all. However, apart from a few lawyers in Calcutta and half a dozen princes, few Indians were bothered about the words of acts of Parliament anyway.

Whilst the renewal of the Charter in 1813 for a further twenty years itself stimulated some increase in the numbers of British people and other Europeans who went to India each year, the gradual change in the Company's role from that of a trading monopoly defended by military establishments into that of the Primary agent of government over enormous stretches of the subcontinent, created acute staffing problems. The debate about the Charter had been confined to Britain. The staffing problem had to be faced in India. So long as the only means of transport between Britain and India remained the long sea route round the Cape, which took up about six months of travel and was costly, and a year for the round trip, the Company was obliged to spread its own personnel, mainly military, very thinly over the ground. This had two direct consequences. The first was that the Company was obliged to draw upon its military regimental officer cadres in order to man a great many civilian posts: administrative, fiscal, judicial and technical, including many medical posts and others in civil engineering. The last named were required for the construction of the major new trunk roads and the making of many canals, used mainly for the distribution of water during the dry season for irrigation of the land for rice, corn, sugar, millets and the many pulses of India. This seriously depleted the officer cadres of the three presidential armies, but especially that of the largest, whose garrisons now were spread at long intervals right across the rural plains of the Indus and the Ganges, in Northern India. That was the army of Bengal.

The second consequence was that the kinds of officers who were withdrawn from their units, often for special courses of training or for civil assignments, included the best all-round officers available. Those left behind in charge of garrison troops tended to be the least able or adjustable of the men who, for that reason alone, were disgruntled. The disgruntled officer is never loved by his own men, shrinking away from them accordingly. Indians, including sepoys, are among the most sensitive human beings in the world.

Villagers had always been attracted by the prospect of service in the armies of the Company, not only by the hope of military victories and the swag which ensued from them, but by its security in the financial sense. Such security was a rare experience for many sepoys who joined the forces, not of the Company, but those of Indian princes who, after a campaign often simply dismissed their forces without either pay or pensions. Whilst the pay of sepoys of the Company was low, even by Indian standards, they felt secure, for they could look forward to a promptly calculated pension based on rank and length of service, and their families would not be left destitute if they were wounded or killed. For these reasons the Company was always able to recruit soldiers, and to select the best available recruits. In order to receive the pay and the highest ranks to which both Indian and British officers could aspire, and thus the highest pensions, there was a strong tendency for officers, British and Indian commissioned and non-commissioned alike, to remain in such ranks till they were far too old for effective command. This became a source of ridicule and, especially on the British side, had lamentable consequences during the Mutiny.

In the year 1830 the first steam-powered ship left Britain for Alexandria with passengers for India who crossed the desert to join another such ship at Suez for the onward voyage. This was the start of the short sea route, of momentous consequence for the future of Indo-British relationships. The new route, together with the total abolition of the Company's trading functions in 1833, soon solved the staffing problem in India, by bringing out hundreds of newly appointed officers, many of them with British wives and children. Such relief, however, was associated with a deep psychological change, whose influence powerfully reinforced the other causes of Mutiny to come.

Wilberforce's enormous speech had expressed two mutually associated trends. The first was overt hatred and contempt for a wide range of age-old Indian customs and beliefs, both Hindu and Muslim. I do not question his horror at such customs and beliefs, but wish to demonstrate its historical importance alone.

The second was his complete assurance, shared by him and all the other evangelists, including Dr Thomas Chalmers himself, not only of the existence of God, but of their own knowledge of His divine will. They knew exactly what God had decided about British policy for India. How did such assurances and convictions come to prevail over the dominant outlook of the previous seven or eight decades of normally intelligent beings of the Western world? I think it is sufficient to say that the new Christian arrogance – for it was nothing less – had been engendered by the powerful military and naval success of Britain in the previous century. The successive waves of British people who went to India after 1830, right down to the beginning of the First World War, shared the same arrogant spirit. The counter-hatred which it produced in the minds of Indian sepoys and other village folk found expression in the events summarized in the next chapter of this book.

Christopher Hibbert (*The Great Mutiny* pp. 54–5) has described the immediate pre-Mutiny epoch in some telling passages:

... Muslims shared with Hindus this fear for their religion. Indeed, the Commissioner for Patna reported that there was a 'full belief' among even 'intelligent natives, especially the better class of Mohammedans, 'that the Government was immediately about to attempt the forcible conversion of its subjects'. The Lieutenant Governor of Bengal considered that the suspicion had taken such deep root that he must issue a proclamation denying it, which, far from subduing the people's fears, served merely to aggravate them.

There had been no such widespread fear in the eighteenth century. The British had been tolerant then. Their officials had contributed to Mohammedan processions; they had administered Hindu temple funds and supervised prilgrimages to holy places; their officers had piled their swords, next to their soldiers' muskets, round the altar at the Hindu festival of Dasehra, to be blessed by the priests. It had been perfectly well understood that the obligations and restrictions of caste imposed upon the Hindu soldier's behaviour were all-important to him, that he would have to throw away his food if the shadow of a European officer passed over it, that it would be better to die of thirst – as some soldiers did die – than to accept a drink from a polluted hand or vessel. But since then all had changed. Indian culture was less inclined to be respected than to be mocked by British officials ...

Rarely scrupling to pull down temples that might stand in their way, the British had brought the so-called wonders of science to India, the electric telegraph, the railway and those steam engines which ... were driven by the force of demons trying to escape from the iron box in which the firinghis (foreigners) had imprisoned them – demons who were, perhaps, the precursors of those devils that, as ancient prophecies foretold, were to rule the world in an accursed age soon to dawn. The railways, the electric telegraph and the steam vessel would bring all men closer, the British said; but that in itself was a threat. For bringing men closer might eventually put an end to caste; and without caste how could a man be rewarded for his acts in a previous incarnation?

... Missionaries, prohibited from working in India in the eighteenth century, now spoke openly of the day when all men would embrace Christianity and turn against the heathen gods; and though it was claimed that the missionaries were not paid by the Government – as the chaplains who cared for the British soldiers and civilians were – their activities were approved of, and in many cases supported by, the Government. So what really was the difference?

Moreover, as the Indians went on to argue, there were plenty of British officers and officials who behaved as though they were missionaries themselves. Colonel S. G. Wheler, commanding officer of the 34th Native Infantry, openly admitted in 1857 that he had endeavoured to convert sepoys and others to Christianity, that he conceived it to be the aim of every Christian, that it was certainly his own object in life, that he always hoped that 'the Lord would make him the happy instrument of converting his neighbour to God or, in other words, or rescuing him from neighbour to God or, in other words, of rescuing him from eternal destruction . . .' His opinions were far from uncommon amongst army officers.

I want next to quote a few passages from Philip Mason's history of the Indian Army and again from Christopher Hibbert, to illustrate the above themes. They were illuminated by the memoirs of an old Indian soldier, Sita Ram Pande, published in 1873 by Colonel J. T. Norgate, who retired in 1880 as a major-general. There are some doubts about the authenticity of the memoirs, but Philip Mason gives convincing reasons for accepting them with generous allowances for the defective memory of an old man and the difficulties of translating into English the words used by the author in a local dialect of Hindi (that of a district in Oudh). The general tenor of the memoirs coincides with the views of many British writers of the period. Sita Ram Pande served for about forty-eight years in the Bengal Army, becoming a subadar (Indian commander of a company of sepoys) at the age of about sixty-five.

Of the earlier period before the new arrivals, both writers quote the same passage in the memoirs:

In those days the sahibs could speak our language much better than they do now, and they mixed more with us. Although officers today have to pass the language examinations, and have to read books, they do not understnad our language . . . The only language they learn is that of the lower orders, which they pick up from the servants, and which is unsuitable to be used in polite conversation. The sahibs often used to give nautches for the regiment, and they attended all the men's games. They also took us with them when they went out hunting . . . Nowadays they seldom attend nautches because their padre sahibs have told them it is wrong. These padre sahibs have done, and are still doing, many things to estrange the

British officers from the sepoys. When I was a sepoy the captain of my company would have some men at his house all day long and he talked with them. Of course, many went with the intention of gaining something . . . but far more of us went because we liked the sahib who always treated us as if we were his children . . . I know that many officers nowadays only speak to their men when obliged to do so, and they show that the business is irksome and try to get rid of the sepoys as quickly as possible. One sahib told us that he never knew what to say to us. The sahib always knew what to say, and how to say it, when I was a young soldier . . .

From Hibbert:

In his young days at the beginning of the century, in contrast to the 1850s, the colonel of Sita Ram's regiment was a familiar figure to everyone . . . He was 'well known all around' as well as in the regiment, Sita Ram said; and 'villagers came from as far as thirty miles away to inform him where the game was' when he wanted to organize a tiger hunt to which he would, perhaps, invite a local land-holder. Contemporaries of his, who appear in other memoirs of the time, wrestled with their men or fenced with them or took them out hawking. One colonel is described as sending a non-commissioned officer ahead of him on the march to discover the best chess players in the village nearest his camping ground. Another, who knew 'how to treat the sepoys in their own way' . . . could make his men roar with laughter or shake in their shoes as he pleased! Like most British officers in India he had a native mistress, and made no attempt to interfere with her ancient faith which he was prepared to respect until God saw fit to change it. *It was not until the 1830s and 1840s, when marriage to white women became more common, that living with a native mistress was considered to be rather disreputable. By then it was 'fashionable' to admire what came from England and to eschew everything 'black'; increasingly the figure of fun became, not the griffin . . . but the peppery colonel with his hookah, his mulligatawny and his Indian mistress!* [My italics.]

The literature of the British Empire, both in India and elsewhere, contains many descriptions of the new arrogance, which often took the form of verbal or physical brutalism on the part of British people of all ranks and vocations, in their dealings, at close quarters, with the people among whom they found themselves. I have italicized the last few lines of the above quotation because such conduct was often rooted in the domestic scene. Women, by nature, are often irritated by ethnic and cultural differences: probably more so than men. British wives, unfortunately, could never be selected for their roles as the partners of responsible men in tropical conditions. Only a few exceptional human beings of either sex were temperamentally qualified for the responsibility of sustaining British prestige in tropical conditions anyway. However, it often happened that a man of no more than average ability in this field was promoted to a sensitive post by virtue of the manifest excellence of his wife as hostess in the world of authority.

The chronology of the Mutiny and of its eventual suppression is very confusing to follow. The reason for this is that the story of the events at each of the principal centres, Delhi, Jhansi Lucknow and Cawnpore, forms a single continuous narrative. There reader of any one of the available accounts (of which I believe that Christopher Hibbert has provided the most vivid of recent years) becomes deeply absorbed by the riveting drama of each, and finds it almost impossible to keep in mind that a similar narrative awaits his attention when he turns his mind to any of the others, and that there is much overlap in the time sequence. Again, retention of a chronological sequence is not simplified by the occurrence of a great many incidents at lesser centres, and of many ferocious battles, some of them in the waterlogged conditions of the Indian monsoon months, fought both in the streets of the towns and out in the paddy fields and burning villages of the Northern plain.

Against such a background of chronological confusion my purpose is to distil from the multiplicity of facts such clues as will enable the reader to explain to himself the main motivation of the mutineers and the state of mind of the British officers and soldiers who managed to defeat them. I have already tried to explain the motivation of the mutineers. Their driving passion was a determination utterly to destroy the British community as a whole, whose image had become hideously miasmic. The British were not merely alien imperial rulers, of which Indians had experienced many varieties in the course of their history. They were an incarnation of absolute evil. Why? Because they would destroy the sacred values of caste, transforming all men into the lowest manifestation of the living, grinding them into the earth of their own Indian land beneath the wheels of the Christian juggernaut. On the British side was the motivation of total retribution, completely vicarious, for the massacres of women and children that had occurred at Delhi, Cawnpore, Jhansi and elsewhere. That at Cawnpore, and that at Jhansi had followed acts of treachery. In the minds of simple British soldiers and of simple people in Britain, massacres, some treacherous, had been committed, not by particular Indians to be identified by any judicial processes, but by 'Indians' in a vague, non-specific sense. '*They*' were guilty. '*They*' should be bayoneted, hanged or blown from guns. 'The whole lot' should be 'wiped out'.

The Events

The Mutiny began at Barrackpore, near Calcutta, in February 1857, and ended at Gwalior in June 1858, about 200 miles south west of Delhi. Between those dates there were a great many incidents including massacres, executions, sieges and bombardments and the movements over hundreds of miles of territory of large bodies of troops, infantry, cavalry and artillery, with all the supporting elements of contemporary warfare. The events constituted full-scale war, whatever other words may be used to describe them.

The southern part of the peninsula was not directly involved with the fighting, but was much affected by the movements of troops, which must have disturbed the life of the whole country.

My purpose in this chapter is not to summarize the events in a continuous narrative, for that would involve more condensation than would be compatible with readability in a short book. I want to describe a few of the main events, in order to familiarize the modern general reader with the kinds of situations in which John Chalmers was occasionally able to pause to write his letters. Chronology, however, is important, to prevent the reader from assuming that he would have been aware of some important event at the time of writing this or that letter, when in fact it had not yet occurred at all.

Spread over the first seven months of 1857, and interspersed with major outbreaks of the Mutiny itself, there were incidents at musketry training centres of the Bengal army at Dum-Dum near Calcutta, Ambala about a hundred miles north of Delhi and at Sialkot, about a hundred miles north east of Lahore. The incidents were concerned with technical changes in the weaponry of the troops, both British and Indian. The muskets to which the sepoys were accustomed were smooth-bored and fired a round projectile a relatively short distance. About ninety years before, however, during the American War of Independence, the value of a new weapon, the rifle, was discovered. The bore contained two slightly twisting grooves and, instead of a ball, a pointed bullet was used. The grooves caused the bullet to spin in flight, to be much more accurately aimed, and to cover a longer trajectory. Both the old smooth-bored musket and the new rifle had to be muzzle-loaded in two operations. First the charge of powder and then the ball or the bullet, had to be inserted with a ramrod. Later, in the 1840s and at the beginning of the 1850s, rifles with two grooves were developed. To facilitate muzzle-loading, lubrication was needed. By 1856 there were many rifle companies among the infantry battalions of the three armies of the Company, and a few whole battalions of British troops were thus equipped.

Associated with the new two groove rifles, the speed of loading was greatly increased. The charge of powder, wrapped in paper, was attached to the base of the bullet to form a package, the whole to be pushed down the barrel in a single operation. The earliest lubrication of the barrels of rifles was by means of a mixture of wax and vegetable oil. It was later found that tallow was better. The new, single package cartridge-cum-bullet was heavily greased with tallow, and the drill provided that the base of the paper cartridge case was to be broken by the soldier, using his teeth for the purpose. This exposed the powder so that it could be ignited by pressing the trigger.

Samples of the new rifles and cartridges had been sent to India in 1853 for experimental use by Indian troops, who had then raised no objections to them. No trouble need have arisen had the tallow been made from the fat of sheep or goats. By 1857, however, cartridges issued to Indian troops did, apparently, contain tallow made of beef or pig fat. At any rate, it was widely believed by Indian troops that they did, and insufficient attention was given to the need for credible assurances about this. How was it possible for the responsible British authorities, either in Britain or in India, to be so insensitive as to allow

Indian susceptibilities to be disregarded? It is much easier to make lists of evident causes of the Indian Mutiny than to provide an answer to this basic question. Merely to say that the British people have 'always' been insensitive anyway is not very helpful. For, however far back one goes into the past of 'always', an explanation will remain to be identified. If we go back to the Garden of Eden, all the characteristics of all the people of the world throughout the past will have to be found in the constitutions of Adam and Eve themselves. For present purposes I shall go no further back than the age of arrogance and its novelty in India nearly two centuries ago.

British insensitiveness is clear when we spell out the facts *as they appeared to the sepoys*. To be forced to touch the fat of a slaughtered cow with his teeth was actually to destroy the caste identity of a Hindu, or to be forced to touch the fat of a pig with his teeth was to destroy the faith of a Muslim. Why should the British decide to set about such wholesale destruction? There could be only one explanation. They were determined to stamp out the religions of India in order that they, the soldiers of their own land, might be made available to fight overseas in all the future wars of the British empire. That could be greatly facilitated if they could be forcibly converted into Christians as fast as possible.

The integrating motivation of the Hindu is the pursuit and preservation of purity. The same word is used by the Christian, but for each the word means something quite distinct. For the Christian, purity implies a conception of the perfection of what he calls body-and-soul. Pursuit of this entity is available to every single human being, irrespective of his or her membership of any particular grouping of humankind. For the Christian there are just two categories, an imaginary God, always available to attend to human prayer, and a completely abstract figure called Man. The Hindu's notion of purity implies the anterior concept of caste. All human beings, with no exceptions, are eternally grouped into castes, hereditary, unalterable, fixed. Each human being, therefore, seeks to embody in his own existence the purest representation of the caste allotted to him at the beginning of the universe. The rules for the pursuit of such purity, transmitted from ancient sacred writings from generation to generation, govern every act of life, including the use of the lips and teeth. In short, Charles Grant, Junior got it right in his speech in the Commons in 1813.

I have stressed the importance of the question of the cartridges, partly because it so clearly illustrates the motivation of the sepoys, and partly because it was associated with several incidents up and down the country. There were many additional factors, however, to reinforce the mood of the sepoys in 1857. The most important of these was the deposition of the Nawab of Oudh and the annexation of his territory under the new name of the North West Province of Agra and Oudh, in 1856, on the grounds of the enduring incompetence and misgovernment of its rulers extending over several decades. This measure was felt as an affront to a great number of the Indian troops of the Bengal Army, who had been recruited among the villages of Oudh. Hitherto, in consequence of the Company's treaty arrangements with the kingdom, extending over many decades, sepoys of Oudh enjoyed various privileges, especially in their capacity as Brahmin landlords in their villages. Such privileges were now almost completely removed. Company rule, however efficient, just and wise by British standards, was no substitute for that of indigenous rulers, however miserable the objective conditions of the peasantry were considered to be by British residents at the Nawab's profligate court at Lucknow, the capital city.

Other measures implied direct interference with traditional Hindu codes: in 1850 a law was enacted to permit a son to inherit his father's property even though the son had changed his religion. In 1856, after much argument, another law made it possible for a Hindu widow (no longer lawfully combustible) to re-marry. This had been opposed on the ground that it would encourage married women to poison their husbands in order to have a chance of marrying somebody else. Other laws also interfered with religious customs: prisoners were obliged to submit to common messing arrangements (though suitably blessed by priests); Muslim prisoners were obliged to shave their heads; brass drinking vessels (*lotas*) were prohibited in prisons because they had been used as handy weapons in brawls, earthenware vessels being issued instead, despite the supposed difficulty of preventing the pollution of the caste of their users. Of this Philip Mason writes: 'The order about earthenware lotas was worse than an order in a modern gaol that everyone must use the same tooth brush; it was not only physically disgusting; it was sacrilegious ... Townspeople sided with the prisoners; there were riots in two places in Bihar' ... in 1855.

A long list of similar factors contributed to the belief that the British would shortly convert all Indian troops into Christians by the use of artillery and bayonets. There was nothing odd about the belief. Islam had often been propagated by similar methods, in India and elsewhere, with manifest success. Why not Christianity? The ghosts of Wilberforce and of the Revd Dr T. Chalmers have a lot to answer for.

The Mutiny is supposed to have originated one day in January 1857 at the musketry training centre at Dum-Dum, eight miles from Calcutta, when a low-caste worker was ill-advised enough to ask a high-caste sepoy for a drink of water from his brass *lota*. The request was refused, at which the thirsty man retorted that high and low caste would soon be abolished, because cartridges smeared with pig and cow fat would soon be in general use throughout the army. The report immediately spread through Bengal and right across Northern India for hundreds of miles. The British had many enemies, including especially several princely rulers who had been deposed in recent years, either because of their inefficiency, or because there was no natural heir, other than an adopted son, whose entitlement to rule had been rejected by the British authority. This was in pursuit of a forward policy of expansion in the power of the Company to administer the land by its own public services. (I have mentioned the case of Oudh on p. 53.) Such former rulers and their followers were suspected of stirring up the sepoys of Bengal to some kind of insurrection. The rumour about enforced conversion of the troops into

Christians was also attributed to them. An organization, the Dharma Sobha, of Calcutta, whose function was to preserve the integrity of Hinduism, was also suspected. There can be no certainty about the conspiratorial factor, however, nor about the precise origins of rumours. Nevertheless, it is hard to see how the similarity of many of the outbreaks of the Mutiny, stretching over about a thousand miles of Northern India, or the timing of them, could have occurred without a conspiracy of some kind.

Apprehension about enforced conversion to Christianity was responsible for mutinous conduct in regiments stationed at Dum-Dum, Barrackpore and Berhampore (the last situated about a hundred miles to the north of Barrackpore, itself quite close to Calcutta). None of these incidents caused much loss of life, but great fear and anxiety was aroused on both sides. At Dum-Dum sepoys expressed their feelings about the cartridges by setting fire to military buildings during the night. At Berhampore the men of the 19th Regiment of Native Infantry, very excited, paraded with their weapons at night and seemed prepared to commit some atrocity. Their British commanding officer addressed them in a blustering manner with threats of dire punishment if they refused to use the new cartridges or the paper in which they were wrapped. The men suspected that a new kind of paper had been somehow saturated with the wrong kind of fat. He decided to overawe the men with the use of horse-drawn artillery at a special parade. To avoid a catastrophe, a group of Indian officers persuaded him to withdraw the guns, which at last he did.

Most alarming to the British side was the fact that between Calcutta and Dinapore, near Patna in Bihar, 700 miles up the River Ganges, there were only two battalions of British troops, the normal garrisons being away in Burma at the time. Orders were hastily given for a British regiment to be sent back to Bengal by sea immediately. They were required for two purposes. The first was to reinforce the authority of the Company in Bengal and across the Northern plain. The second was to be present on parade at Barrackpore when the mutinous 19th Regiment was to be ceremonially disbanded as punishment for their misconduct at Berhampore. The British reinforcements were at sea when the disgraced 19th were marching down to Barrackpore for the grim ceremony.

News of the impending arrival of the British unit spread rapidly all over Bengal and was wildly misinterpreted. The men now believed that the British troops were intended, not for the humdrum task of forcibly converting thousands of Indian sepoys into Christians, but to exterminate them altogether by way of punishment for their incendiarism and mutinous behaviour at Berhampore about the cartridges. When the dreaded parade actually took place, with the British troops smartly lined up before the far more numerous sepoys, the men of the 19th were silent with seeming contrition but also trembling with fear. The disbandment is thus described in the standard work on the Mutiny:*

As the morning dawned upon them, obedient to orders, they commenced the last march that they were ever to make as soldiers. Heavy-hearted, penitent, and with the remains of a great fear still clinging to them, they went to their doom. A mile from Barrackpur Hearsey met them with his final orders, and placing himself in front of the column, rode back with them to the parade ground which was to be the scene of their disbandment. There all the available troops in the Presidency division, European and Native, were drawn up to receive them. Steadily they marched on to the ground which had been marked out for them, and found themselves face to face with the guns. If there had been any thought of resistance, it would have passed away at the first sight of that imposing array of white troops and the two field batteries which confronted them. But they had never thought of anything but submission. Obedient, therefore, to the word of command, up to the last moment of their military existence, they listened in silence to the General's brief preliminary address, in silence to the General Order of Government announcing the sentence of disbandment; without a murmur, opened their ranks, piled their arms at the word of command as though they had been on a common parade, and then hung their belts upon their bayonets. The colours of the regiment were then brought to the front, and laid upon a rest composed of a little pile of crossed muskets. It was an anxious moment, for though the 19th were penitent and submissive,

*Sir John Kaye and Col. G. B. Malleson, *History of the Indian Mutiny, 1857–8*, Cabinet Edition, 1888, vol. 1, pp. 399 *et seq.*

the temper of some of the other regiments, and especially of the 34th, was not to be trusted; and for a while it was believed that the men, who two days before had thrown off the mask, were prepared to fire upon their officers. The rumour ran that many of the Sipahis of that guilty regiment were on parade with loaded muskets, and Hearsey was advised to prove them by ordering the regiment to spring ramrods. But he wisely rejected the advice, saying that all was going well, and that he would not mar the effect of the peaceable disbandment of the regiment by a movement that might excite a collision. He was right. The work that he had in hand was quietly completed. The men of the 19th were marched to a distance from their arms, and the pay that was due to them brought out for disbursment. They had now ceased to be soldiers; but there was no further degradation in store for them. Hearsey addressed them in tones of kindness, saying that, though the Government had decreed their summary dismissal, their uniforms would not be stripped from their backs, and that as a reward for their penitance and good conduct on the march from Barhampur, they would be provided at the public cost with carriage to convey them to their homes. This kindness made a deep impression upon them. Many of them lifted up their voices, bewailing their fate and loudly declaring that they would revenge themselves upon the 34th, who had tempted them to their undoing. One man, apparently spokesman for his comrades, said, 'Give us back our arms for ten minutes before we go; and leave us alone with the 34th to settle our account with them.'

Whilst the men of what had once been the 19th were being paid, Hearsey addressed the other Native regiments on parade, very much as he had addressed them before; but urging upon them the consideration of the fact that the 19th, in which there were four hundred Brahmans and a hundred and fifty Rajputs, had been sent to their homes, and were at liberty to visit what shrines they pleased, and to worship where their fathers had worshipped before them, as a proof that the report which had been circulated of the intention of Government to interfere with their religion was nothing but a base falsehood. The men listened attentively to what was said; and when the time came for their dismissal, they went quietly to their lines. It was nearly nine o'clock before the men of the old 19th had been paid up; and, under an European escort, were marched out of Barrackpur. As they moved off, they cheered the fine old soldier, whose duty it had been to disband them, and wished him a long and happy life; and he went to his house with a heart stirred to its very depths with a compassionate sorrow, feeling doubtless that it was the saddest morning's work he had ever done, but thanking God that it had been done so peacefully and with such perfect success.

(Major-General Hearsey was the divisional commander of the troops in Bengal, the brigadier in command of the garrison at Barrackpore being Charles Grant.)

During the few days before the disbandment of the 19th on 31 March, sensational incidents had occurred near the guard room of the 34th at Barrackpore, where a Brahman sepoy of the regiment, Manghal Pande, had conducted a one-man mutiny on his own. Marching up and down before the guard room and brandishing his *tulwar* and loaded musket, he had challenged the troops to rise and kill the British officers. The troops did not respond, but the men on guard did not arrest him either. When a young British officer, the adjutant, appeared, Pande attacked and wounded the officer and his horse. General Hearsey himself and his two sons, both officers of the regiment, suddenly appeared on the scene and demonstrated total fearlessness of Pande and his loaded musket. The men looked on sheepishly. Pande, sensing the total failure of his mutinous appeal, turned his musket upon himself and fell to the ground. He recovered in hospital, but was rapidly court-martialled and hanged. The whole incident was sufficiently grave to cause the flight of many British women and children to Calcutta. In all the circumstances the disbandment of the 19th had been a very risky business. If the men had not been contrite, and if the men of the 34th had not been very wary, and if any man less courageous and cool-headed than General Hearsey had been in command a massacre could easily have occurred.

A little later the 4th also was disbanded. Roaming disbanded sepoys, though deprived of their weapons, must have contributed to a general sympathy for the mutineers in the villages of Northern India.

During the period of the mutiny British soldiers, including John Chalmers, referred to the mutineers as 'Pandies'.

The incidents described so far, though quite minor ones compared with those to follow, provided a seed bed for the latter, the first of which occurred at the military depot and bazaar town of Meerut beginning on 24 April 1857, at the height of the hot weather. Here again the use of cartridges was the spark.

At Meerut there was a full division of troops, including British units, the 1st Battalion of the 60th Rifles, the 6th Dragoon Guards and some artillery: about 1,700 British troops altogether, amounting to a little less than half the total number of Indian troops belonging to various units. In the cantonment were many British wives and children.

On 24 April ninety men of the 3rd Light Cavalry, an Indian unit, were paraded and ordered to take up three cartridges each. With the exception of five men, three Muslims and two Hindus, all the rest refused to obey the command, despite assurances that the paper of each might be torn with the fingers instead of the teeth. The eighty-five men who had disobeyed orders were taken off duty and sent back to the lines, pending a court of inquiry into the incident. The Judge Advocate General advised a court martial, which was duly held. All but a few of the men were sentenced to ten years hard labour in the prison, and led off in iron shackles. A few of the men were given shorter sentences. The extremely severe sentences led at once to an uprising of sepoys and sowars (cavalrymen), who were joined by a large rabble of civilians from the bazaar, armed with various weapons. Several British officers and soldiers were shot dead. Several of their wives were murdered and their bodies mutilated. A great many buildings were set on fire at night, and the mutineers succeeded in releasing the prisoners and hacking off their shackles. Most of the mutineers then set off across country to Delhi, but for various reasons they were not followed by British troops or any loyal Indian contingents. An important reason for the failure to pursue and destroy the mutineers was that many of the British troops were new to the country and already showing signs of exhaustion in the extreme heat, which, at that time of year, persists all through the night.

It is very clear from the story of Meerut that, at each critical stage, the situation hovered between order and massacre, the outcome depending heavily upon the personalities and conduct of responsible British officers, who were worn out by long years of service in India without recuperative leave. Such men, in their bewilderment, were either far too severe or too soft at moments of extreme danger.

It is important to record that the sepoys included a large number who, throughout the events at Meerut, remained loyal to their British officers and their wives, protecting them against the mutineers and against armed hooligans from the bazaar.

The main chronological question, in my view, is the timing of the main massacres. The massacre of Europeans at Delhi took place as early as 11 May 1857. The slaughter at Cawnpore took place on 27 June. At Delhi the assaults leading to the ultimate British victory took place in September 1857. Lucknow was not finally reconquered till 2 March 1858. At Cawnpore the mutineers were finally crushed early in December 1857. This sequence means that, at each of the main defeats of the mutineers, when hundreds of Indians, whatever part they had actually played in the massacres or the treachery, were killed by the bayonet thrusts of Scottish and English soldiers – and of many Indian soldiers who fought with them against the mutineers – or were hanged in hundreds from the trees, or blown from the muzzles of guns, the victors carried in their minds the images of those massacres. Such images were exaggerated by gross elaboration of fictitious detail, including the rape of women and their mutilation. During the battles themselves British troops were ferocious, yelling of Cawnpore as they hacked and stabbed at any Indians who stood before them or lay beneath their feet. No mercy was sought or given: helpless old men were butchered, and many Indian women, too, were killed. As for British officers, several of them, including Havelock and Neill, were convinced that vengeance was the motive of God Himself. In many an officers' mess the man who expressed concern about the morality of retribution found himself scorned by his superiors. Genocide may never have been effective in the story of religious war, but in the suppression of the Indian Mutiny our forebears rejoiced in the blindness of their deeds.

Delhi

We should avoid identifying the aims of the mutineers of 1857 with those of Indian nationalists of later decades in the century or with those of the Indian National Congress of the Mahatma Gandhi and the Nehru dynasty in our own epoch. For the mutineers were not aware of any such notion as nationality, with its concepts of national territorial boundaries and constitutional autonomy, flags, emblems and anthems as subsequently manifest in the world at large. For them there was no world at large anyway. Their aim was to preserve an ancient identity beyond any formal definition. However, when we come to the events at Delhi, it is clear that feelings generically related to modern nationalism did indeed motivate them.

Despite the historical importance of Delhi itself and the momentous nature of the events there, neither are difficult to summarize quite briefly, which cannot be said of the other main events of the Mutiny period. In this chapter the length of my summary of each event bears no relation to its intrinsic importance, but reflects the complexity of the task.

We can only guess why the mutineers at Meerut, after their effective demonstrations of incendiarism and homicide, set off across country to Delhi, though many of them drifted away to their own villages, where they remained. On the British side, at every stage, ample documentary evidence of motivation at each stage is available in the military records and the writings of participants. The mutineers, however, included very few literate individuals. Hence the guesswork required for interpretation.

The very name of Delhi evokes images of sovereign power going back into a distant past, beginning about the end of the tenth century A.D. The recorded history of India coincides pretty closely with that of Western Europe, and the notion of a vaster period of known history is quite chimerical. Thereafter the site became the seat of a succession of Muslim dynasties until the first of the Moghul emperors, Babur, ruler of the Afghan uplands, established his power in India at Delhi early in the sixteenth century. By the middle of the nineteenth century the last of the Moghuls, known simply as the King of Delhi, was an old man of over eighty years of age, in a state of amiable dotage. He enjoyed no power but lived on a pension of about £10,000 a month granted by the Company. In the old palace, the Red Fort adjoining the Jumna river, he lived in some luxury. The king, Bahadur Shah, was the son of a previous Muslim Moghul ruler, but his mother had been a Hindu, a Rajput princess. The old man was in no sense a religious fanatic, having no objections either to Hindus or Christians. In his youth he had been a great hunter and fine marksman, and in his later years he had enjoyed Indian classical music. He had laid out beautiful gardens and had always been fond of animal pets. He was regarded as a civilized old gentleman, treated with courteous deference by the Company's military officers whose job it was to guard and look after him. The principal trouble was that the palace was crammed with his relatives, near and remote, some prosperous, others virtually destitute, so that no pension could ever be enough for his needs. Financing them was about as impossible as financing the British national health service today. Supply is always less than demand, which is infinitely elastic.

Sir John Kaye, the major historian of the Mutiny, believed that, on their journey from Meerut, the mutineers must have lived in desperate fear of the British troops, the 60th Rifles and the unit of a Guards regiment who, they assumed, must be following hard upon their heels, determined to shoot or hang every one of them in a fury of vengeance. The great walls and ramparts of Delhi, both those surrounding the city and the even bigger walls of the Red Fort within it, would afford strong defences against any avenging British.

Kaye's theory is convincing. We do not know what the mutineers thought about the old king himself. Judging by their subsequent acts I think they envisaged him as a living embodiment of the Moghul dynasty of the past, before which their ancestors had bowed in obeisance, and were probably quite unaware of his true nature as a very old human being. Such notions would endow their actions in Delhi with a 'national' objective: to restore their own emperor to his rightful position at last, by exterminating the hated foreign Christians who ruled their land in his stead.

Their attitude, I believe, was deeply Indian, differing fundamentally from that of revolutionaries in the Western world. In the West the endless processions of revolutions which constitute our history can be seen, however tendentiously, as 'class struggle'. Revolutionaries are envisaged as overthrowing the authority of preceding dominant classes. Had the mutineers at Delhi followed the Western model they would have proclaimed *themselves* as the new rulers: 'We, the People!' (always furnished with capital letter and exclamation mark). Looking back on them, we should have imagined the military *sansculottes* as they advanced into the future with banners unfolding into the wind, accompanied by a few voluptuous female figures whose saried torsos recall the splendour of monuments in the cities of South America. The reality was otherwise.

The first of the mutineers to arrive from Meerut were the cavalrymen, the sowars, on their horses. The infantry, the sepoys, followed a few hours later. The horsemen rode up to a spot beneath the windows of the king's apartments and shouted up to him an appeal for assistance in their fight 'for the faith'. The king made no reply but sent the commander of his bodyguard, Captain Douglas, to speak to them. Addressing them from a balcony, Douglas ordered them to go to an old palace just outside the city and wait there whilst their claims were considered. In the meantime, they must leave the palace area, where their presence was vexatious to His Majesty.

The mutinous cavalry ignored Douglas's orders and went into the city itself through one of the gates that was open. Massacre then began. Within a few hours on that day, 11 May, most of the British officers of the large military cantonment close to Delhi, and all those attendant on the king were hacked to pieces by razor-sharp sabre cuts. The worst outrage was committed against a group of about fifty civilian Christians, most of them women, including a number of Eurasians, and their children. All were dragged to an open space beneath a tree, bound together with a rope and then slashed to death by sabre cuts. The bodies were piled into bullock carts and taken to the bank of the Jumna, where they were flung into the river, for the satisfaction of the gharials (Indian crocodiles).

Within a few days all the sepoy units of the cantonment near the city rose in mutiny, killing their British officers, their wives and children. When the entire British position at Delhi had become indefensible, a group of British artillery officers found a way of blowing up the largest magazine of small arms, shells and grenades in India, thus preventing the contents from falling into the hands of the enemy. In the colossal explosion four of the officers lost their lives. A number of mutineers were also killed by exploding shells and cartridges. A small number of British officers and soldiers, together with some of the wives and children, managed to escape at night through a hole in one of the fortress walls, lowering themselves down to the bottom of a rampart of soft soil and then struggling up the other side to the top. This they did under constant musketry and rifle fire. They were then shielded by thorny jungle, without food, water or shelter from the blazing sun. Many died in the ensuing weeks of desperate wandering, their bodies eaten by vultures, jackals or swarms of insects. Some reached villages where the people mocked them, but in others kindly villagers, at grave risk to themselves, fed and cared for them. Many spent months disguised as Indians, and eventually survived altogether. Their memoirs form a considerable literature of the epoch.

Delhi was not recaptured from the mutineers by the forces of the Company until towards the end of September 1857. In India the dry weather begins with the end of the monsoon about mid-October, and ends in June the following year after weeks of intense heat and humidity. Many of the mutinous uprisings occurred during the dry, increasingly hot months of the year, and the subsequent monsoon created great difficulties for troops of all arms in their slow movements in waterlogged countryside for the relief of fortified urban centres which had been seized by the mutineers in the earlier arid and torrid months.

As we shall see, it was in the relief of Delhi that John Chalmers was himself most dramatically involved.

Lucknow

Lucknow, former capital city of the rulers of Oudh, stands on the south bank of the River Gumti, a tributary of the Ganges, about 120 miles upstream to the north west of Allahabad and 60 miles north east of Cawnpore. The state had been feudal territory subject to the Moghul emperors of Delhi, but had in practice been virtually independent for many decades. For about a century before the Mutiny the Company had maintained friendly relations with the nawabs of Oudh, who welcomed British military protection against rival princes, despite the cost of it which they were obliged to pay to the Company. They were glad, too, to trade with the Western world on a considerable scale. Many thousands of the men of Oudh were recruited into the battalions of the Bengal army: indeed, just before the Mutiny they constituted almost half its total manpower. Whilst the rulers of Oudh were Muslims, most of the troops recruited into the Company's Bengal army were Hindus, and a large proportion of them were men of the higher castes, Brahmins and Kshatryas (the princely or warrior caste). In the event of disputes about their holdings and miscellaneous rights vis-à-vis their Muslim rulers, they were able to call upon their British officers in support of their claims. Such support the latter were often able to provide by taking up their cases with the British resident at the court of Lucknow. He, in turn, would approach the prince.

Looked at from a cultural standpoint, Lucknow was of much interest. Whilst its rulers had never been to Europe, they admired the palatial architectures of European ruling dynasties, as they imagined them to be. The nawabs had for a hundred years engaged European architects to erect similar structures at Lucknow and to lay out fine parks and ornamental gardens reminiscent of Versailles or Hampton Court. In Europe hard limestone is available, but in the Gangetic plain hardly any stone existed. The buildings were actually made of bricks, but the local people discovered how to cover them with very hard plaster, so that they resembled the pillared palaces of Europe, even at close quarters.*

Successive Governors-General in Calcutta faced a persistent problem in their dealings with Oudh, a problem also experienced with the rulers of other princely states with whom they were associated by treaty. The very extent of British authority in the subcontinent was felt by the British to endow them with responsibility for the welfare of all the inhabitants, whatever the consitutional position might be. For, unless the British accepted such responsibility, their imperial dominion could have no moral justification. The evangelical values of the mid-Victorian age dominated British concern about their position in India, but especially in Oudh.

The nawabs, for generations, had been grossly tryannical, exacting revenue from their peasantry at the point of the bayonet and squandering the proceeds on their own vicious luxury and sloth. The British resident at Lucknow, Sir William Sleeman, wrote vivid reports for Lord Hardinge, the Governor-General. Here are a few quotations:

> The Talookdars [revenue farmers] keep the country in a perpetual state of disturbance, and render life, property and industry, everywhere insecure. Whenever they quarrel with each other, or with the local authorities of the Government, from whatever cause, they take no indiscriminate plunder and murder ... no road, town, village or hamlet, is secure from their merciless attacks – robbery and murder become their diversion, their sport, and they think no more of taking the lives of men, women and children, who never offended them, than those of deer and wild hogs.

The Nawab maintained an army of about 80,000 men in addition to the force supplied by the Company. Sleeman writes:

> Three fourths of the officers commanding the regiments are singers, eunuchs or their creatures, or the creatures of the court

---

*An excellent account of the architectural phenomenon of Lucknow is provided by Dr Rosie Llewellyn-Jones in her book *A Fatal Friendship: The Nawabs, the British and the City of Lucknow*, Oxford University Press, 1985.

favourites . . . ! The troops upon which the collectors of the revenues depend are amongst the worst enemies the people of the country have. They dare not face a formidable landowner or gang of robbers, but are ever engaged in pillaging the farmers and cultivators of the land, and this with the knowledge of the Government and its officers.

What the people want, and most earnestly pray for . . . is that our government should take upon itself the responsibility of governing them well and permanently. All classes save the knaves who now surround and govern the King, earnestly pray for this – the educated classes because they would then have a chance of respectable employment, which none of them now have, the middle classes, because they find no protection or encouragement, and no hope that their children will be permitted to inherit the property they leave, not invested in our own government securities; and the humbler classes, because they are now abandoned to the merciless rapacity of the starving troops and other public establishments, and of the landholders driven or invited to rebellion by the present state of misrule.

Sleeman, however, did not recommend the annexation of Oudh. As Sir Penderel Moon summarized his views: 'Sleeman recommended . . . that the British should assume the administration as trustees for the Royal family and people, spending the whole of the revenues for their benefit and distinctly disclaiming any pecuniary advantage. "If we do this," he said, "all India will think us right!"'

Although the Directors in London left to the discretion of Governors-General the decision as to what ought to be done about Oudh and other incompetent Indian states, the Company was so preoccupied by wars in Burma, Sindh, Afghanistan and central India as to be unable to settle the matter till 1856, when the ruler of Oudh was summarily deposed and his entire territory taken over by the Company. Sleeman and other administrators had strongly opposed the policy of annexation and conquest of Indian princely states. Here is his reasoning:

The system of annexing and absorbing Native States – so popular with our Indian services, and so much advocated by a certain class of writers in public journals – might some day render us too visibly dependent on our Native Army; that they might see it, and that accidents might occur to unite them, or too great a portion of them, in some desperate act ... The Native States I consider to be breakwaters, and when they are all swept away we shall be left to the mercy of our Native Army, which may not always be sufficiently under our control.*

Prophetic indeed. Dalhousie was the Governor-General mainly responsible for the take-over. His action was the main proximate cause of the Mutiny of the following year, in Lucknow itself.

The British community at Lucknow, both military and civilian, was widely scattered over miles of territory, in military cantonments, urban shops and scattered residences, some private, some official. Sir Henry Lawrence, elder brother of the great Sir John Lawrence of the Punjab and later Viceroy, had been appointed to the job of Commissioner of Oudh at Lucknow after the take-over by the Company in 1856. Himself a lifelong soldier of distinction, and fully expecting mutiny at Lucknow among the various sepoy units in the cantonments, Lawrence decided to concentrate the European community as closely as possible in the large British Residency and among the nearby official and private residences. Every civilian, including Italian and French shopkeepers, was trained to use a rifle and to man every defensible position, night and day. The banqueting hall of the residency was made into a makeshift hospital for wounded.†

The first mutinous outbreak occurred at Lucknow in April

---

*From Sir Penderel Moon, *The British Conquest and Dominion of India*, London, 1989, pp. 648–9.

†Since writing the above paragraphs I have read with great interest the recently published biography of Sir Henry Lawrence entitled *Lawrence of Lucknow* (1990) by Sir John Lawrence Bt. OBE, who is a great-grandson of Sir Henry. It is clear from the book that, whilst Lawrence correctly anticipated the mutiny in Northern India and the siege of Lucknow itself, at which he was himself killed, his own deeply religious feelings were such that it could never have occurred to him that the primary cause of the Mutiny was the evangelical movement itself. He believed that the main causes lay in defects in the structure of the Bengal army and the deprivation of promotion prospects for Indian soldiers, however able they might be, compared with those of British military personnel. He was right about this and was a strong supporter of Sleeman's views about the annexation of Oudh. The mutineers were defeated largely because they included very few officers able to take effective tactical or strategic command, or to undertake effective staff work.

1857, after which the European community were under siege, almost continuous, day and night, until the final relief came towards the end of March 1858, when the last rebels were dislodged. The siege was lifted briefly by General Havelock with his very small army in September 1857, but then resumed again until it was finally relieved by Sir Colin Campbell the following year. During the siege hundreds of men, women and children were killed outright by shells bursting through the walls of the residency, or by bullets crashing through the windows. Little girls had their heads blown off whilst playing with their dolls, little boys were blown to pieces playing at mutineers. Women were killed saying their prayers or whilst getting into bed. The clothing of men, stinking and sweat soaked, was torn to shreds during skirmishes in the surrounding jungle. Women made up clothing out of the tattered garments left by men who had been killed. As all consumable goods from the bazaars were exhausted, prices rose and people spent all their remaining money in buying something to smoke or to drink. During the hot weather horses and bullocks died of thirst, their carcases creating an unbearable stench. Parties of men went out at night and did their best to bury them, at considerable risk to themselves. The banqueting hall was full of gangrenous, dying men, the whole place a stinking hell. And then, when the great rain came, together with the wind, parts of the residency collapsed, burying men, women and children beneath the ruins; the graves of dead animals were opened by the water, insects and disease spread apace. Dying men in the hospital insisted on staggering to the windows to fire at least one shot at the mutineers before they died.

Throughout the grimmest events of the Mutiny we can trace the persistence of the evangelical consciousness of the British community as a whole, both among men and women. General Havelock himself was a devout Baptist, totally confident that his determination to exterminate every rebel or mutineer upon whom he could lay his hands, irrespective of his responsibility for any specific crime, coincided with the manifest will of God Himself. So also was Colonel Neill, the grim avenger at Cawnpore. The memoirs of many of the women include their prayers to God, any doubt as to whose existence was quite inconceivable. However few the conversions effected by the evangelists, it was their motivation itself that the mutineers themselves were determined to destroy.

Jhansi

Jhansi was the name of a small princely state in North West Central India, just to the south of Gwalior and north west of the large area of Bundelkhand. The whole region forms a northern extremity of the Deccan, a hilly region rising from the Gangetic plain. It was also the name of its capital city, fortified since the early seventeenth century by massive walls and a powerful fort within the town. Its history had been that of a bastion of the predominantly Hindu world to the south of the Moghul power at Delhi. At the time of the Mutiny the area of Jhansi had been about three hundred square miles, and its population about a quarter of a million.

In 1732 the principal leader of Bundelkhand, whose name was Chhatra Sal, sought the help of the Peshwa, head of the Mahratta state in Western India, in resisting attacks by the forces of the Moghul power to the north. In recognition of such assistance, Chhatra Sal ceded to the Peshwa the territory and citadel of Jhansi, whose local ruler bore the title of subadar, or commander.

In 1817 the Mahratta Confederacy was overthrown at the close of a series of complex military campaigns led by Britain in alliance with various Indian rulers.* The consequence was that Britain succeeded the Peshwa as the paramount power over all the previously tributary states of the Peshwa, including Jhansi. Such was the *de facto* situation, whatever may have been the *de jure* and constitutional position.

The British continued to recognize the subadars of Jhansi and their heirs, receiving their tribute in exchange for such recognition and British military protection during a turbid

---

*The almost unreadable complexity of the campaigns is described in pp. 568–73 of the *Oxford History of India* (third edition). The story of the state of Jhansi, and of the Rani herself, is lucidly narrated by D. V. Tahmankar in his book *The Ranee of Jhansi* (London, 1958).

period of Indian history. In 1832 the Governor-General, Lord William Bentinck, visited Jhansi where he conferred upon the subadar the title of maharajah (rajah for short), in recognition of the soundness of his administration and of his loyalty to the paramount power. In 1825 the subadar had sent his own forces to assist the British in dealing with a minor mutiny in central India. The name of the subadar was Ramachandra Rao. During the first Burma war (1824–26) Ramachandra Rao's support for the British had taken a quixotic form when he advanced the sum of Rs. 70,000 to assist the British war effort and later declined to accept any repayment.

In November 1853 the reigning rajah, Gangadhar Rao, died, leaving no offspring. His widow, the rani, who belonged to a Brahmin Mahratta family, the Tambes, at a town called Wai in Mahrashtra, had married him in 1842 as his second wife when she was a girl of fourteen. Her name had been Manakarnika, but on the occasion of her marriage she had been given, instead, the more illustrious name of Lakshmibai, after Lakshmi, goddess of wealth and success. Lakshmibai gave birth to a male child, but it had died in infancy, so there was no direct male heir for the state. Shortly before he died the rajah had adopted a Brahmin boy of high aristocratic descent, Damodar, aged five, in the hope that the rani would be recognized by the British as regent for the boy, and that the dynasty would thus be secured.

Having regard to what occurred later, it is significant that, before her marriage to the rajah in 1842, she had been strongly recommended to him as a suitable wife by no less a person than the aged former Peshwa, Bajee Rao II, who was living on his pension in his palace at Bithoor, near Cawnpoor. Bajee Rao had adopted a youth, Dondo Pant, later known as the Nana Sahib, and it is very clear that the Rani of Jhansi and the Nana Sahib shared a common resentment against the British power, over the treatment both received.

After the death of the rajah several responsible British officers at Jhansi and elsewhere, in reports to the Governor-General, had strongly recommended that the claims of the rani both to act as regent for the boy Damodar and to administer the state should be accepted, both in deference to what appeared to be universal Indian opinion and tradition, and to her personal fitness for such responsibilities. Owing to the absence of Dalhousie on tour, the fatal decision about Jhansi was not taken by him until 27 February 1854. She was then told bluntly that her dynasty was at an end and that she would receive a pension of £6,000 per annum, out of which she would be required to settle the debts of the late rajah. Indeed, deductions were made from her pension for that purpose.

Incensed at the decision, she sent petitions to the Governor-General and to London, protesting her case, entirely in vain. The arrogance and insensitivity of the British authorities at the highest levels seems in retrospect manifest, not only in respect of Jhansi but of other states taken over by Dalhousie in the middle of the century. As for Jhansi, its rulers, from the beginning, had been wholly loyal to the British power, and there was absolutely nothing in her conduct to lead Dalhousie to expect anything but such loyalty on the part of the rani herself. The word arrogance implies a condition of blindness to the consequences of decision.

Troops of the Bengal army of the Company formed the garrison at Jhansi. They included a detachment of Foot Artillery, part of the 12th Regiment of Native Infantry and parts of the 14th Irregular Cavalry. All were Indian troops, commanded by British officers. There were no British troops at all, and the garrison amounted to several hundred men in all. They were stationed in the military cantonment area a short distance from the city. Captain Dunlop, of the 12th Native Infantry, was in command. The political and administrative officer at Jhansi was Captain Alexander Skene.

Within the area of the cantonment was a small structure known as the Star Fort, which contained the Company's treasure chest, and artillerymen, with their guns, were stationed there.

Shortly after the mutinous events near Calcutta, at Meerut, Delhi and Lucknow in the first few months of 1857, the rani sought the permission of Captain Skene to raise a body of her own troops, for her personal protection, presumably against possible mutinous risings at Jhansi, and she was given such permission readily. She also dug up some guns which had been buried secretly after the death of her husband, the rajah.

Within the old, massive fort of Jhansi were stationed a miscellaneous group of British officers, part military and part civilian, with Eurasians and virtually all the women and children of the Europeans of all kinds, and their servants.

Neither Captain Skene, Captain Dunlop nor most of their colleagues appear to have expressed any apprehensions about possible mutiny at Jhansi. Suddenly, however, as at Meerut, fires broke out at the bungalows of various British officers in the cantonment area, but they were assumed to have been caused by accidents. On 5 June mutiny began. A company of the 12th Native Infantry, led by an Indian sergeant, marched into the Star Fort and declared their intention to hold it. The remaining companies of the 12th, however, made no moves and expressed their disapproval of the action of the mutinous company. I shall not give a description of what happened next because, as is common in such situations, there were conflicting accounts of the events. Captain Dunlop was shot dead by his own men after walking to the post office to post some letters. On the following day, 6 June, all the cavalry and infantry troops rose. Several British officers were killed. The remainder managed somehow to escape and make their way into the main fort in the city, where they prepared at speed to defend the inhabitants. Then followed a siege by the mutineers, joined by the recently raised force of the Rani. The position of the defenders was desperate. Colonel Malleson describes it thus:

Rifles had been distributed; the ladies told off to cast bullets and to cook; piles of stones had been piled up behind the gates, and positions allotted to each member of the garrison. When, therefore, the rebels approached the fort, they were received with so well directed a fire that they fell back in confusion to prepare renewed efforts for the morrow. The resources now available to the besiegers lay in the guns which the Rani had unearthed. During the night these, and smaller *matériel* from the cantonment, were placed in position ... A successful defence seemed impossible. Guns, provisions, a continued supply of water, were all wanting. It was decided, then, at the council [of war] to send three of the garrison under safe conduct to treat with the Rani for the retirement of the men, women and children within the fort, to a place of security in British territory.

Three British emissaries issued from the fort. They were seized by mutineers and taken to the palace. I shall not quote Malleson's account of their treatment by the rani, because it is contested by other authorities. The emissaries were murdered and the siege continued. On 8 June messengers arrived from the rani offering safe conduct for the defenders and their escort to another station under British control, if they would lay down their arms. They agreed to do so and left the fort accordingly. The rebels immediately bound them with ropes into three groups, men, women and children, and moved all of them into a garden called the Jokan Bagh. Then, suddenly, the officer in charge of the prison raised his sword as a signal and the entire community of the former defenders were butchered. One man only, whose name was T. A. Martin, managed somehow to escape. Tahmankar (*op. cit.*) quotes a letter from him to Damodar Rao (the adopted son of the rajah) about the rani, written years afterwards (1889):

Your poor mother was very unjustly and cruelly dealt with – and no one knows her true case as I do. The poor thing took no part whatever in the massacre of the European residents of Jhansi in June 1857. On the contrary she supplied them with food for two days after they had gone into the fort – got a hundred matchlock men from Kurrura and sent them to assist us, but after being kept a day in the fort they were sent away in the evening. She then advised Major Skene and Captain Gordon to fly at once to Datia and place themselves under the Raja's protection, but even this they would not do; and finally they were all massacred by our own troops.

The number of those massacred at Jhansi was between sixty and a hundred altogether. It is a very small number compared with the number of Indians who were killed during the suppression of the mutiny. The British community in India was small anyway. The numbers of Indians available to experience a colossal revenge was limitless.

Jhansi was not recaptured by the British until 3 April 1858, under the command of Major-General Sir Hugh Rose. The rani escaped and joined forces with another of the rebel leaders, Tantya Tope. She was killed in battle against British troops on 17 June. The details of her death are as variously reported as the events of the massacre of the previous year. On occasions when the entire community of a besieged place are killed, who remains to describe the events?

The precise responsibility of the rani for the massacre can never be determined. British and Indian historians, however, are virtually unanimous in their tributes to her qualities of statesmanship, administrative acumen, beauty and charismatic leadership in a desperate war. Her treatment at the hands of the British authorities is deplored by almost all the authorities, British and Indian.

Cawnpore

Cawnpore (now Kanpur), unlike other principal centres of the Mutiny, was a city which owed its existence entirely to military considerations. Situated on the west bank of the Ganges its location became of great importance as the Company's main forward base in numerous campaigns in central India and to the west and south. The most important of such campaigns had been waged in alliance with the nawabs of Oudh against the Mahrattas, who overran the territories of the Moghuls. Others were fought against Gwalior (a hundred miles to the west), against the Sikhs of the Punjab and various powers to the south. It was the largest cantonment in India, stretching for six miles along the riverside.

Around the cantonment had grown up a commercial and industrial city, full of shops containing the latest products from England and Europe generally, from pots of orange marmalade, ladies' hats, veils and corsets to the most fashionable carriages. There were fine assembly rooms, clubs, a racecourse, churches, hotels, and a huge Indian bazaar. The population included a large Eurasian element, and Christians of many kinds. All these people were merging into the universal caste system of Indian society, a process of integration that was tragically ended by the Mutiny and its outcome.*

In 1857 the cantonment held a garrison of four Indian regiments – three of infantry, one of cavalry – and a company of artillery, about 3,000 men in all. There was no complete British regiment but about 300 British military personnel altogether, most of them officers of the Indian units, about sixty gunners with six short-range guns, a few NCOs and

---

*See Zoë Yalland, *Traders and Nabobs: The British in Cawnpore 1765–1857* (1987). In addition to her account of the social background, Mrs Yalland provides, I believe, the finest short account of the mutiny at Cawnpore available.

miscellaneous other Europeans of the commissariat, medical and similar ancillary groups. There were about 300 women and children.

The senior British officer at Cawnpore was Major-General Sir Hugh Wheeler, a man of sixty-seven. The son of a captain in the Company's forces, he had been born in Ireland, educated briefly at Bath Grammar School and commissioned into the Company's forces at the seemingly incredible age of fourteen. He spoke several Indian languages with complete fluency, was devoted to his Indian troops and to the life of the country. He had an Indian wife and two daughters. Held in wide respect among both the British and Indian communities, he was expected to become Commander-in-Chief of all the Company's forces on the retirement of General Anson.

By the middle of May the British community at Cawnpore lived, day and night, in a state of continual fear. Wheeler was fully aware of the danger but his position was exceedingly difficult, because any obvious preparations for defence must be evident to all the Indian troops, and could spark the threatened insurrection. However, he believed that, if the troops mutinied, they would not bother to kill off the British community at Cawnpore but, like their fellow mutineers at Meerut, would go off to Delhi as fast as possible.

He set about building an earth rampart about four feet high, with a ditch of about the same depth, right round an open area containing two large barrack buildings normally used for British troops. One of them had a straw roof, but the larger one, built of bricks, was more durably covered. The earth rampart was manned with every available man able to use a musket or a rifle, and by the six guns of the artillery. Virtually all the women and children, and a good proportion of the commercial community of Cawnpore, were assembled within the rectangular ramparts of the earthworks. Stores of food and other supplies were assembled from the town and the bazaar to last for several weeks, and kept in the barrack buildings. Many of the commercial and industrial community left the city disguised as Indians, staying in friendly villages, or preferred the limited security of private residences, which they attempted to defend themselves. Such was the setting.

A dozen miles upstream, on the same side of the river as Cawnpore, is the ancient urban centre of pilgrimage for the Hindus, Bithoor. In 1818 the last of the Mahratta marauding chiefs, Bajee Rao, Peshwa of Poona, was defeated by the forces of the Company. He was given a large pension and allowed to live in his palace at Bithoor under the courtesy title of Maharaja of Bithoor. As already mentioned, he had adopted a son called Dondo Pant, whose caste origins are not recorded. He was known, however, as the Nana Sahib, and widely regarded as the Maharaja's heir. When Bajee Rao died in 1851, however, the British decided that the Nana had no entitlement to the pension formerly paid to the ex-peshwa. The Nana had petitioned the British government about this and had sent a representative to London for the purpose. Despite his grievance, his enormous debts and the unaffordable size of his retinue, he had acquired a reputation for great courtesy to Europeans, whom he entertained lavishly, and among whom he was popular. It is clear, however, that despite his friendship with Europeans, he found himself allied with the mutineers, who looked upon him as their leader. His precise responsibility for the massacres of Europeans and Christians which occurred at Cawnpore can never be known, for, in the last fighting, he managed to escape and disappeared for ever. He could never, therefore, be brought before a court. The important historical point about the Nana is not the extent of his guilt, but the fact that virtually the entire British and Eurasian community believed, without the smallest doubt, that he was responsible for a kind of treachery so heinous as to demand physical vengeance of the utmost savagery. Cawnpore provided the occasion for that savagery, which pursued the mutineers to their own extinction.

The mutiny at Cawnpore began on 5 June. In an extraordinary act of faith (for which presumably General Wheeler was responsible) the Nana's own troops had been allowed to take charge of the Government's treasury at a nearby suburb of Nawabganj. The first incident occurred when the sowars of the 2nd Cavalry rode off to Nawabganj where, helped by the Nana's men, they broke into the treasury after killing the subadar-major in charge of the guard. They unlocked the local jail, let out all the prisoners and set fire to many buildings. Then they went off to the magazine, situated on the river bank to the north west of the town, and seized the contents, a rich store of ammunition both for small arms and for the guns of the artillery company, who soon joined in the mutiny.

Quite apart from the very small number of British troops available to General Wheeler, the grimmest feature of his defensive system of earthworks was that it could only be used during the days of the hot weather that remained before the onset of the monsoon rain – say three weeks at the most. After that the whole place would be turned into a morass of mud and water, impossible even to stand in and totally indefensible. In such conditions no musketry could be used from the ramparts, cartridges would be wet and accurate aim frustrated by blinding rain. In the meantime the defenders of Cawnpore were exposed throughout to the scorching sun all day, and to appalling heat all night. Their skin was cracked and blackened by the sun; thirst was unquenchable, water almost unobtainable. Both in tropical Africa and throughout South East Asia the heat which precedes the annual rain, and the weight of the rain itself, are impossible to imagine by those who have never experienced either.

The most devastating damage by the mutineers at Cawnpore was achieved by the company of artillery, which kept up an almost non-stop bombardment, day and night, directed mainly at the two barrack buildings. The straw roof of the one was soon on fire and collapsed, leaving the interior exposed to the sun. The larger, brick building, crammed to capacity with women and children, was pounded with heavy ball shot almost continually. Dead women and children lay everywhere in gushes of blood. Those not overcome by grief or madness cooked the food of the men at the earthworks and carried it out to them under fire, or made bandages for the wounded, whose injuries were often gangrenous and seething with flies. Occasionally a wall of masonry would collapse, burying men, women and children beneath the rubble of bricks, the air full of rising, suffocating dust.

As for the men at the ramparts, the accuracy of their fire, both with the guns and the musketry, was felt to such effect that mutineers soon became reluctant to attempt any assault upon Wheeler's earthworks. To approach such desperate defenders was to court the eye of deathly aim: better to creep back to the town, where loot and slaughter could be enjoyed with little risk.

The scene in the town was chaotic. Breaking into shops and houses, the mutineers dragged out anybody who appeared to be a European, Christian or Eurasian and hacked him or her to pieces. Every roadway was littered with mutilated corpses. Every inflammable building was set on fire, everything of value stolen. The Nana Sahib appointed one of his adoptive brothers, Baba Bhat, to be a sort of presiding judge at Cawnpore. He at once restored old Hindu practices of mutilation of offenders and of prisoners, and appointed another man to be Superintendent of Supplies and 'given authority to imprison those unwilling to do business with him'.*

Back at the earthworks it was impossible to bury the dead. Before the siege was over 250 bodies had to be taken out beyond the rampart and dropped down a deep well, where they remained.

The imminent death of almost all the British human beings who were involved in the final phases of the events at Cawnpore, and the disappearance of the Nana himself a little later, no doubt explain the slightly varying reports of the final scenes. Broadly, however, what happened was this. On 25 June a woman emissary of the Nana arrived at the earthworks with an offer of respite for the defenders. The woman was reported to have been a Christian. Her written message for Sir

*Christopher Hibbert, *The Great Mutiny*, p. 179.

Hugh Wheeler stated that, if the defenders were to hand over their guns (artillery) to the Nana, all the surviving British community would be given safe conduct down to the river bank, about a mile away, where boats, together with provisions, would be made available to take everybody down stream to the British garrison port of Allahabad. At first Wheeler was disposed to reject any such capitulation, and several officers supported him, determined to defend the position to the last. Eventually, however, he decided to accept the offer because the situation was completely hopeless and the sufferings of the people unbearable, hunger and thirst alone causing death every day. It was agreed that the evacuation should begin early the following morning.

The great concourse, partly on foot, part on stretchers, some on the backs of elephants, some in palanquins, slowly wound its way down to the river bank about a mile away. As they reached the river they had to move into a narrow way lined by buildings and steep banks. On either side of them stood hundreds of mutineers, nearly all of them armed. Suddenly, as though at a signal, the mutineers struck, within a few minutes of reaching the waterside all save four of the men were killed, including General Wheeler and all his officers, his wife and one of his daughters. The four survivors got away because they were strong swimmers, and were eventually rescued by a friendly rajah.

The other daughter of General Wheeler, whose name was Ulrica, became the subject of an interesting story. Years later it became known that an Englishwoman was living as a Muslim in the bazaar. A Mrs Emma Clarke and her husband had settled in Cawnpore in 1880. She arranged for a woman servant (ayah) to go occasionally in a carriage into the bazaar and to bring back to her house the mysterious Englishwoman, who enjoyed wearing European clothes beneath her *burka* (a garment which conceals the whole of a woman's body except for her eyes). Mrs Clarke, who was almost the same age as Ulrica Wheeler, had lived in Lucknow before the mutiny and had probably known Ulrica when they were both girls and the Wheeler family had been stationed there. Ulrica was reported to have been carried off by a Pathan sowar during the massacre, forcibly converted to Islam and married to him. She seems to have told Mrs Clarke that she had been well treated by her husband. She is supposed to have died about the year 1907, when she would have been sixty-seven years of age. It is not known whether or not she had any children.*

About two hundred women and children who had not been killed at the waterside were rounded up and, after various moves, were shut into a single, bungalow-like building called the Bebee Ghur, which had been used in the past as the home of the Indian mistress of a British officer. Here they were confined for many days without sanitation, with very little food and in conditions of severe heat. Many were wounded and some had suffered cruel injuries, such as the tearing of their ears from which mutineers had ripped off jewellery. Ragged and bleeding, many died in the appalling conditions. The mutineers, panic-stricken about the inevitable approach of British avenging forces from various directions, were at first uncertain what to do about the helpless hostages. Suddenly, however (to what extent the Nana himself was responsible can never be known, though most British people were convinced that the decision must have been his), men with sabres entered the building, and began cutting them down, or else they were killed by being fired on through the windows. The bodies were dragged out and flung down a well until it was full. It was reported by Indian observers that many of the women and children were still living when thrown down the well, and that their moans were audible for several days. All the bodies that could not be thrown down the well were loaded into bullock carts and flung into the Ganges.

Cawnpore, devoid of Europeans, remained in the hands of the mutineers for almost six months more, till it was recaptured in extremely bloody hand to hand fighting in the first week of December 1857.

In the preceding summaries I have not attempted to describe the very complex movements of troops that were involved in

*See Zoë Yalland, *Traders and Nabobs*, pp. 324–5.

the numerous campaigns to defeat the mutineers. For my purpose is merely to give the modern reader a simple narrative sufficient for what is likely to be his own interest. As I see it the dominant feature of the entire epoch was something I shall call double genocide. The term is defective, because the mutual extermination of entire communities has occurred very seldom, if ever, in the course of human history. I use the term to indicate the quality of the motivation, not its consequences. It is dramatic enough for practical purposes.

The mixed force of British and Indian troops who eventually re-entered Cawnpore were commanded by Brigadier-General James George Smith Neill, a leader of fiery temper, military and evangelical. He announced that he had for long pondered about the treatment to be applied to captured mutineers at Cawnpore, having regard to the massacres and treachery which had occurred. He decided that they must be made an example (before God) to India and to the world at large. Close to the site of the Bebee Ghur he erected a row of gallows. Close by he accumulated piles of lumps of raw beef and pork, suitable for consumption by orthodox Hindus and Muslims respectively. Parties of rebel prisoners, whether or not, as individuals, they had in fact had anything to do with the massacres, were forced to kneel down upon the stinking floor of the building and to lick up all the dried blood of the women and children with their tongues. Having swallowed sufficient quantities, lumps of beef or pork were thrust down their throats, to enhance their awareness of their own religious propensities. The ceremony completed, all were hanged before great crowds of onlookers. The proceedings lasted for several days.

Sic transit gloria mundi.

John Chalmers: 1821–1859

The writer of these letters from India belonged to a large Scottish family. He was born, however, at Sherborne, in Dorset in Southern England, where his father Patrick was a land agent, an estate administrator, on behalf of the owners of the Lewisham Park estate, a local property. His mother Harriet was the daughter of an Irishman, Mr Carige, who was another land agent in Dorset, having had a similar position in Ireland some years before. Apart from John, their eldest child, there were two other younger children, Eliza and Helen. John's Scottish kinsfolk referred to him as 'English John'.

Patrick was one of the younger sons in a family of fourteen brothers and sisters, and his forebears had belonged to similarly large families. The Chalmerses were country gentlefolk in Scotland, but few of them were 'landed gentry' in the sense that they presided over estates or lived entirely upon their rents as landowners. The progenitors of the largest families were clergymen, whilst many individuals were merchants or manufacturers in small East Coast towns and ports. Some were officers or midshipmen in the Royal Navy or the mercantile marine. Following a strong Scottish tradition, most of the Chalmerses and the families with whom they were associated by marital links attached much importance to secondary, higher or technical education. As educated men and women they were eligible to marry into the landed gentry itself, and the genealogical tree overleaf is intended to show this. Their social stratum, therefore, was not that of a hereditary caste corresponding to a caste in the Hindu society of India, but that of the British élite as a whole. That élite had grown steadily in numbers, authority and self-confidence with the expansion of Britain as a modern state between the end of the seventeenth century and the beginning of the nineteenth, largely by virtue of phenomenal success in war. There had, of course, been the severe defeat of the American war of the 1780s and the loss of the mainland American colonies. But more important for Britain had been the international conflicts of the Seven Years War (1756–63) and the Napoleonic Wars recently ended. It was people like the Chalmerses who filled the professions, the controlling managerial positions in industry and commerce, and the public services, especially in India and the growing Empire overseas.

Apart from Harriet, Mr Carige had another daughter, Mrs Copper, who seems to have been a successful hostess at Wishaw in Lanarkshire, a few miles south east of Glasgow, in the valley of Clyde. There, in 1825, the Clydesdale Distillery had been established by Lord Belhaven who was on the lookout for a good man to manage it. We do not know how Lord Belhaven got to know about Patrick Chalmers, but it could have been a consequence of his acquaintanceship with Mrs Copper. Anyway, Patrick, Harriet, the children and Mr Carige all travelled to Wishaw and Patrick soon acquired the lease of the distillery from Lord Belhaven and made a great success of it.

In 1830 John Chalmers, then nine years old, was sent to Edinburgh to live with the family of one of his father's brothers, Charles Chalmers, and to attend the famous Merchiston Castle School, of which Charles had been the founder and was now the headmaster. At school John showed talent in the 'practical mathematical departments' and it was these skills which characterized his subsequent vocational life in India.

In her biographical sketch, Isabel Grace Chalmers describes the events of John's career after leaving school with a regrettable vagueness about dates and the identities of important individuals in his life. Here is her account:

His education ended, John Chalmers joined his father at the distillery at Wishaw. At this time he was over six feet in height, and well made. His blue eyes and fair curling hair set off a face not otherwise handsome. After getting some insight into the business at home, he was despatched to Ireland, with a view to his gaining experience, and at the same time extending their connection in that quarter.

This was his first taste of independence, and one can well imagine

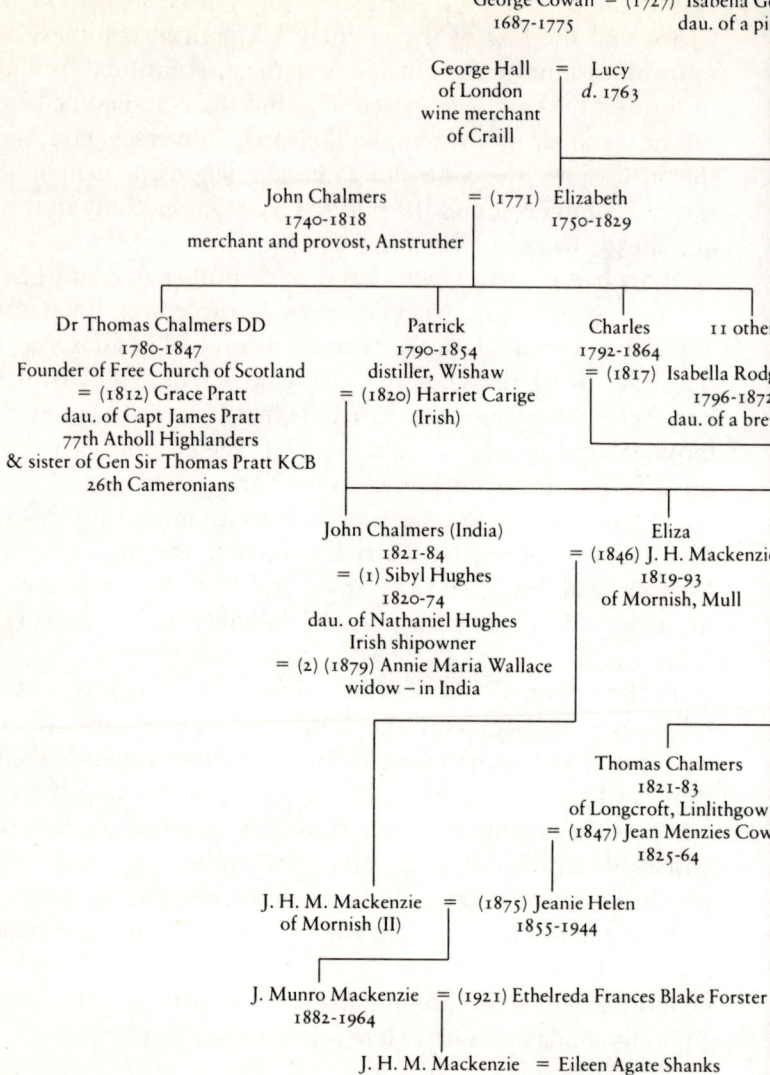

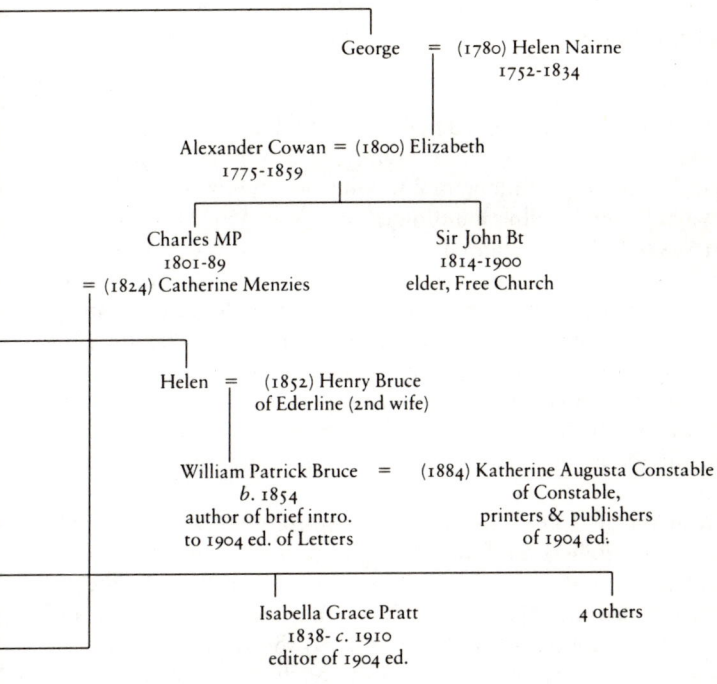

with what eager hopefulness he looked forward to the journey, little knowing that he was hastening to meet the tragedy of his life. Business was neglected amongst the charms of Irish hospitality, but alas! among his many true, generous, warm-hearted friends, there was one of a different mould, the impecunious father of many daughters, who had no intention of bestowing favours on the lad without exacting payment, and more than payment, to the uttermost farthing.

John returned home, engaged to a woman many years older than himself. He soon after married her, and settled down near his father at Wishaw. Time passed. The aggressive economy of his wife's management perhaps blinded him to what was going on, so that the crash when it came wellnigh unhinged him. When his father sent for him and asked for an explanation of bills for goods ordered in the name of 'Mrs Chalmers', he was aghast. On his way back to his own house, other revelations were made to him by a clerk in the office, which filled him with despair. He could not face his trouble, the unknown depths of it. He fled from home and enlisted.

The suspense of his parents, until they found out what had become of their son, was most painful; and to his mother, who was so proud of him, the shock of knowing her son to be a private soldier was terrible.

Mr Mackenzie, John's brother-in-law,[*] offered to visit him in the barracks and see how he fared. He gave a graphic account on his return of the way the men treated the new recruit. He was already their master, their beloved master. When the visit was at an end, and John was to accompany Mr Mackenzie to the station, his willing servants were in attendance ready to fetch and carry. In fact, Mr Mackenzie found they did all the menial work for John that they dared.

He paid one visit to his mother after this. For her sake he petitioned to go home in plain clothes, but whether this was granted or not is not known. It was not long before he was bought out of the army.

The above account is highly derogatory both to John Chalmers's father-in-law and to his wife. Miss Chalmers omits to mention many details that could have been important for the story in this phase in the lives of the couple. Such details

---

[*] John Hugo Mackenzie had married John's elder sister Eliza. He later took over the distillery from Patrick Chalmers with no less success, and subsequently acquired his own estate at Mornish, on the north west coast of the Isle of Mull, together with Calgary Castle, from which the settlement of Calgary in Alberta derives its name.

would include the name of the wife and her age. She describes her as 'many years older than John', which is not good enough. She omits the name and vocation of the father, the date and place of the marriage, the name and date of birth of their child (whose identity appears in one of the later letters). She does not say when John joined the Army nor when he was bought out. She does not say what happened to him after he left the Army and before he was recruited, in Britain, into the Corps of Sappers and Miners of the Bengal Army. Finally, she does not specify the nature of the offence which the wife committed and which was whispered to John by the clerk.

At the time of writing her biographical sketch, probably just after the turn of the century, John's first wife, her father and John himself had all been dead for many years.

Details of births, marriages and deaths in Scotland are kept in the General Register in Edinburgh. I accordingly went there and spent a day at the registry. The law about the national registration of births, marriages and deaths, which came into force in England and Wales in 1838, was not applied to Scotland until 1855. Such details before that date are kept on microfilm at the registry, but, as yet, they are not identifiable unless the particular parishes in which they occurred can be identified.

I made a guess that John Chalmers and his wife would have been married in one of the parishes of the district of Wishaw, in which there are three parishes. I examined the microfilm records of all three parishes but was unable to find any details either of the marriage or the birth of the child Harriet Anne. Since there are a great many other parishes in which the events might have occurred, I decided to abandon the search and try another clue.

It looked, from the wording of Letter No XXVI, as though the first name of John's wife was probably Sibyl. I knew already that, on the occasion of his second marriage in the Punjab in January 1879, he had described himself as a widower. I looked, therefore, at the Scottish national registrations of all female deaths, going backwards from 1878 to 1855. I found that, throughout those years, only one female with the name of Sibyl Chalmers had died — in January 1874. I sent, therefore, for the handwritten record on microfilm. To my delight I found that she is described as the wife of Captain John Chalmers of the Indian Army. Her father was Nathaniel Hughes (deceased), a merchant and ship owner. The details had been reported to the registrar by her brother, whose surname was Hughes, but his first name is not legible from the handwriting. She was said to have been fifty-four years of age when she died, and the cause of her death was reported by the doctor as an ovarian tumour, to which he had added 'many years apoplexy'.*

If Sibyl was indeed fifty-four when she died (and why should we doubt it?) she would have been born in 1820, only a few months before John, so she was not 'many years older' than he, as Miss Chalmers had asserted.

It seems to me fair that without further evidence to justify her castigations we should take a different view of the whole business. We should assume that Sibyl Chalmers, a very young wife and probably the mother of an infant, in the manner of innumerable other young wives since wives began, ran up some bills for others to pay. If she was pretty, which may be assumed without reluctance, she may have been spotted by the clerk doing something flirtatious one evening when moonlight glistened upon the waters of the Clyde.

If Sibyl had not behaved as she did, or if John had been less uptight about it, he would probably have succeeded his father in the management of the distillery, and his achievement in that capacity could have been celebrated eternally on the tubular walls of London Underground stations.

The rest of this book describes another kind of destiny. Having banished himself from the world of his ancestors and contemporaries, we may safely assume that he would never have lost an awareness of their eminence in Scottish and British life. In one of the letters he refers to himself as 'the scamp' of the family. Such a thought would not have occurred

---

*The Hughes mentioned in the first paragraph of Letter I was probably his brother-in-law. The 'Mr' Hughes mentioned in the second line of Letter II was probably his father-in-law.

to him had he not carried in his mind an image of family distinction. The most distinguished of his father's family, of course, was Patrick's elder brother, the Revd Thomas Chalmers, DD, whom I have already described. There is evidence, in some of the letters written after the Mutiny, that John was to some extent motivated by that dominant personality whose name, however, he does not mention. The great evangelist had already died before the Mutiny occurred.

The vagueness of Isabel Grace's account may be largely explained by the unlikelihood that she had any access to records now available at the India Office Library and the Public Record Office in London. She probably relied upon the memories of other members of the family with whom John had corresponded in the past, quite apart from the letters with which she was dealing. I have been able to discover the following facts.

John Chalmers enlisted as a private soldier in Belfast on 20 October 1847. The records in the India Office Library do not show the name of any regiment or corps. Some time in the year 1849 he arrived at one of the Indian ports, in the troopship *Northumberland*. Within a few weeks of his arrival in India he joined a course of training at the Thomason College of Civil Engineering at Roorkee, in the Punjab. The course was one of a series, each of which lasted nineteen months, and his name is included in the list of successful examinees for the year 1851. We do not know the starting or ending dates of the course. At the time of his qualification as a civil engineer his substantive position was that of a corporal in the '2nd. Cy. Sappers and Miners'. I have ascertained from the Public Record Office that that abreviated description means that he was a corporal in the 2nd Company of the Royal Corps of Sappers and Miners, a British formation which preceded the Royal Engineers.

I found that the 2nd Company of the corps (there were over twenty companies scattered about the world) was stationed at Gibraltar in 1848 and 1849, and that John's company officer was a Captain Hutchinson. So far as I could gather, no part of the Company was stationed in India at all. The troopship *Northumberland*, bound for Bengal, sailed from Portsmouth on 13 June 1848, and carried the 10th Royal Regiment of Foot.

The above records still leave unclear how Corporal John Chalmers came to go to India. A little reflection, however, suggests the following hypothesis. At some stage after his enlistment in Belfast, his company commander Hutchinson decided that John Chalmers possessed the educational background to qualify him to attend the course at Roorkee in India. He was therefore ordered to join the troopship *Northumberland* either at Portsmouth or Gibraltar, and to report to the Thomason College in the Punjab as soon as possible after getting to India. He was 'bought out' of the Sappers and Miners early in 1852, presumably by his father, who would have been delighted to learn that his son had at last become a professional man and a gentleman, after all. Dr G. Thomas, of the Search Department in the Public Record Office, concurs. He told me, moreover, that the records of members of infantry and cavalry regiments, especially relating to service in India, are much fuller than those of sappers and engineers.

The India Office Library possesses no records of his postings as a civil engineer until 1856, when he is described in the index to a Bengal directory as the executive engineer in charge of the first section of the Lahore-Peshawar trunk road, then under construction by the Punjab government. He was stationed at Gujranwala, from which place the first of the letters in this collection were written. The librarians suggested that, if any of such records still exist, they will be held by the authorities in Delhi. I am not delaying the publication of this book to conduct correspondence about such details. It is clear from certain passages in the letters that, during the four years between 1852 and 1856, he was not confined to Gujranwala but had other jobs at other places, all in the Punjab.

The above paragraphs suggest that John Chalmers married Sibyl Hughes some time between 1845 and 1846 or 1847, and that it was within that short period that Sibyl ran up the troublesome bills and, probably, gave birth to the child Harriet Anne.

When Isabel Grace says that 'it was not long before he was bought out of the army', she overlooks the considerable period between the date of his enlistment in Belfast in 1847 and the date when he resigned 'by purchase' early in 1852. She gives the impression that he was already an officer when he went to India, which was not so.

By way of a tailpiece to this chapter, I want to mention the possibility of interesting links between the Chalmers and Mackenzie families of Scotland and the famous French Protestant royal family of Condé, and the city of Calgary in Alberta, Canada (see the footnote to p. 90). A surviving member of that family is His Royal Highness Major-General A. B. A. de Bourbon, Prince of Condé, who lives in Tangier, who has been in correspondence with Mr Mackenzie and with myself about such connections.

The city of Calgary goes back to the year 1883, before which the locality was inhabited by Indians only. The first non-Indian settlement was given its name of Calgary, after Calgary Castle in the isle of Mull, by a Colonel Macleod, who was a brother-in-law of Mr Mackenzie's great-great-grandfather, of Mornish, in Mull, the husband of John Chalmers's elder sister Eliza, of Wishaw of the 1840s. The Prince of Condé's middle name is the Scottish name of Bruce, and he has forebears whose names included Chalmers and Cowan (see the genealogical tree), some of whom lived in Calgary, Alberta from the 1890s onwards. In the city there is a Chalmers Presbyterian church, founded in 1957 and named after John Chalmers's famous uncle, the Revd Dr Thomas Chalmers, DD, and there is also a Grace Church, named presumably after his wife Grace Pratt. There are several families of Chalmers in Calgary today, but all their forebears seem to have arrived from other parts of Canada or from the United States. It seems very likely that links with the Chalmers family discussed in this book exist, but the difficulties of tracing them in detail today are formidable, for the name of Chalmers is quite common throughout the English-speaking world.

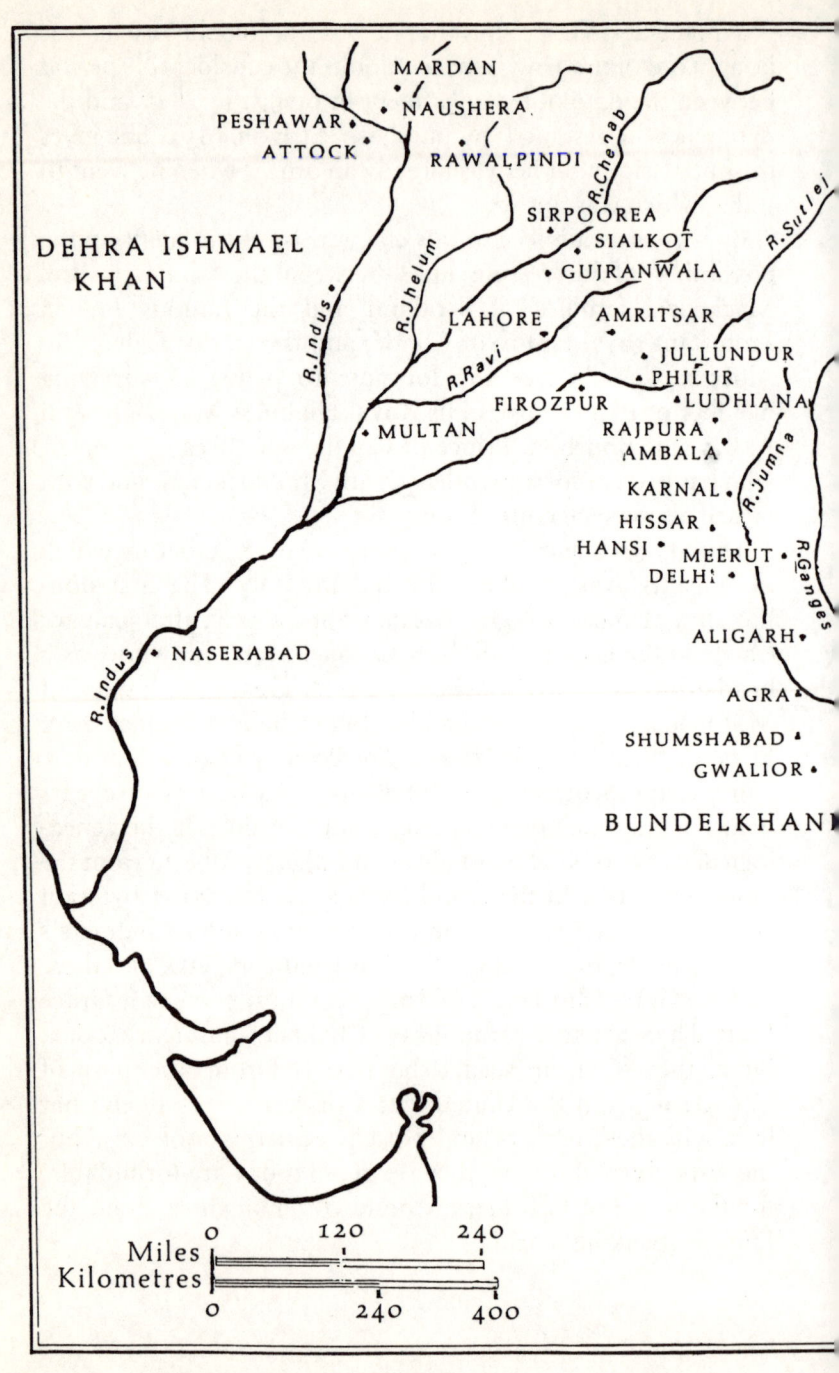

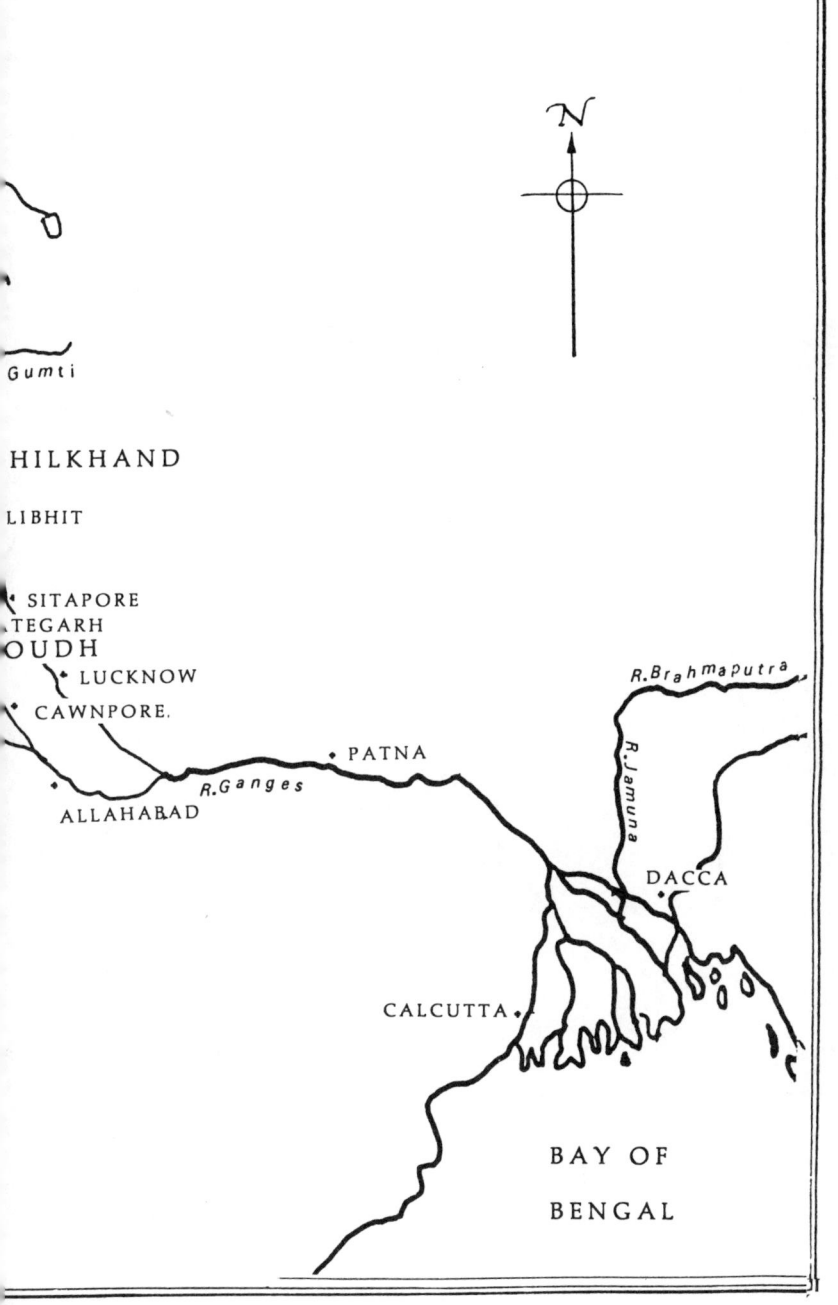

The Letters

In this book I am including all the letters published in the edition of 1904 that were written during the period of the Mutiny and for some months after it was over. I am excluding the later ones about the Waziri campaigns because they concern a different subject and events belonging to a subsequent phase of Indo-British history.

The following letters were written between 30 May 1857 and 15 November 1859. When reading them, I recommend the reader to refer back occasionally in order to ascertain how their chronological sequence relates to that of the most traumatic events of the Mutiny itself, namely, the massacres of Europeans at Delhi, Jhansi and Cawnpore. For to do so will enable him to imagine which of such events were known to John Chalmers at the times of writing. Such knowledge illuminates his emotions as they shifted in the passage of time. Here I am referring to the massacres only, and not to the long, protracted agony of Lucknow, where it was the mutineers themselves who were finally massacred by British and Indian soldiers.

The sequence of the principal massacres was: Delhi 11 May 1857; Jhansi 8 June 1857; Cawnpore 27 June 1857.

The principal battles in which the mutineers were defeated occurred on the following dates:

Last rebel strongholds at Delhi captured: 20 September 1857

Final defeat of the rebels at Cawnpore: 6 December 1857

Last rebels dislodged at Lucknow: 20 March 1858

Jhansi captured and sacked: 3 April 1858

Death of the Rani in battle: 17 June 1858

I now quote the letters, adding a few comments below any of them which may require elucidation for the modern reader.

LETTER I

GOOJERANWALLA, 30th May 1857.

My dear John,

Since the last mail our communications have been cut off for some time, but it is hoped they are now open. However, to secure some news, I have written a few lines at intervals of some days, first to Bruce, next to Hughes, and now to you, and sent them by different routes, in hopes that some one or other would go safe, but, from what I hear to-day, the others have all been kept back at the Lahore post office until all was safe on the route, and will go with this.

You must have heard by the last mail of the massacres of Merutt and Delhi, and no doubt have felt that I also was in a mess. Well, things did look bad enough here, and are far from clear yet, but here we have had no murders, but some hard fighting at Ferozepore and Murdan, near Peshawur, with the mutineers. At the latter place, when the 55th N. I. rose, their Colonel, Col. Spottiswoode, one of my oldest friends in the Punjaub, was so much distressed to think his regiment should do so, that he committed suicide.

General Anson, the Commander-in-Chief of India, has died; the newspapers say of cholera, private reports say suicide. He, from his ignorance of the country, had raised a storm that has already cost hundreds of English lives, and may cost us India, and when done he was not the man to meet it.

In the Punjaub we have met the rebels fairly – beaten them at every point, and sent a large force of about 1000 men from the Punjaub, and a lot from the hills to relieve Merutt and Delhi. Brigadier-General Chamberlain, a splendid young fellow, commands, and is in the room as I write, talking about the affair. The army is passing here yesterday and to-day, making forced marches.

From the newspapers you will hear horrid accounts of the Delhi affair, but the one half will never be published. The brutes oiled over and set fire to one lady, killed children at the breast; and 50 ladies and children who got into the palace of the king, who, the rascal, was put on the throne by us, and has received £12,000 a month of pension for years, were, after remaining there 5 days, stripped naked, paraded through the crowded streets of the largest city in India in that state, under a burning sun, and then killed with spears slowly and in cold blood – ladies and children who never knew what it was before to walk a mile. Never mention this to those who might have had friends there, but it is true, as I have seen the Government report; but the retribution will and must be heavy, both on the wretches who have committed, and on the Court of Directory who have by their mismanagement caused, such horrors.

Love to all, and believe that I am at present as safe as any man with an English face can be in India; and believe me, my dear John, your aff. brother, JOHN CHALMERS

How I regret that I ever left the army, as I would give freely 10 years of my life to strike a blow against such wretches, and as an engineer I am floored, as the amount plundered from the treasuries, and the expense of this affair, will stop all works of our sort for years to come.

LETTER I

Gujranwalla is about forty miles north of Lahore and about 250 miles north west of Delhi as the crow flies, but much further, of course, on the ground.

The letter is addressed to John Monro Mackenzie, who had married his elder sister Eliza.

He refers to events at Ferozepore, Murdan, Peshawar and Naushera, all of which lay in a district of strategic importance on the routes through the mountains into Afghanistan. A few years before, in the First Afghan War (1839–42), Britain had suffered serious reverses, consequences of the over-confidence in which the campaign had commenced, and it was feared lest mutinous uprisings among the Company's troops stationed at those places might lead to support for them from tribesmen beyond the frontier. It was this fear which had prompted severe action in dealing with such mutinous events as did occur near the frontier and in the Punjab generally. Chalmers shows awareness of the dangers ahead for the entire British position in North Western India.

As for the suicide of Colonel Spottiswoode, like many other commanding officers of sepoy battalions in the Bengal Army, he could not believe that his own troops, of whom he was so proud, were about to mutiny and must therefore be forcibly disarmed as a preventive measure. Just before he shot himself he had been offered support by a body of loyal Sikhs and Punjabi Mussulman troops should any conflict with mutinous sepoys, mostly Hindus, including many from Oudh, occur, but he refused to accept it. His act and attitude was characteristic of the early days of the Mutiny.

Major-General the Hon. George Anson, the Commander-in-Chief, did not commit suicide, but had died of cholera at Karnal, about sixty miles north of Delhi. He was succeeded as commander of the forces at Delhi by Lieutenant-General Sir Henry Barnard, who also died of cholera of 5 July 1857, during the operation to recapture the city from the mutineers. Until a vaccine was discovered during the Second World War, cholera was one of the most appalling scourges of South East Asia. It is a water-borne intestinal disease whose symptoms are incessant diarrhoea, dehydration of the entire body and excruciating pain. The average period of time between the onset of the first pain and death is about eleven hours. The disease is spread rapidly throughout a district by swarms of flies.

In this and subsequent letters Chalmers mentions individuals whose subsequent careers were distinguished, and it is clear that he knew some of them personally.

It seems probable than in no other generation of British history did so many dominant personalities, many of them military officers, contribute more powerfully to the character of the epoch in every field of endeavour. I do not think this was a consequence of mere chance, and that two factors were mainly responsible for it. The first was the prevailing imperial arrogance I have mentioned earlier. The personalities were dominant, authoritarian figures in a milieu of values conducive to their emergence. The second was the social environment of India herself which, throughout history to the present day, has been deeply adulatory towards the powerful decision-makers of the highest castes.

He mentions Brigadier Chamberlain, 'a splendid young fellow', who was in command. Chamberlain, born in 1820, was about the same age as Chalmers (born in 1821). He had joined the Bengal Army in 1837 at the age of seventeen. After distinguishing himself in the Afghan War, during which he was wounded several times, he had become Military Secretary to the Governor of Bombay (1846–7) and ADC to the

Governor-General in 1847. In 1850 he commanded the Punjab Military Police, and had become the Commander of the Punjab Frontier Force in 1854–7. In 1857 he became Adjutant General of the Indian Army (that is, of all three of the armies of the Company) and was thus largely responsible for the successful siege of Delhi later in that year. As a field-marshal he was Commander-in-Chief of the Madras Army in 1876. His full title, at the time of his death in England in 1902 was Field-Marshal Sir Neville Bowes Chamberlain, GCB. His last job in India had been that of Military Member of the Council of the Governor-General.

LETTER II

GOOJERANWALLA, 13th June 1857.

My dear Bruce,

Last mail I wrote to you, to Mackenzie, and to Mr Hughes, and as everything is all right in Bombay, I have no doubt all the letters reached safe enough. I will now send you an account of how things stand here, and perhaps if you were to send the letter to Wishaw and Kilwinning, it might be acceptable.

Below Lucknow we have no information, but there two Native Infantry regts. and one Cavalry regt. have mutinied and gone off to Seetapore, a notoriously disaffected district. In Cawnpore all is right at present, or at least by the last accounts. At Agra the Native Infantry and Cavalry regts. are disarmed, the European reg. and Artillery being strong enough to have done so. At Allygurh, Futtygurh, and Nusserabad the native troops have mutinied, but most of the Europeans have escaped. At Hansi and Hissar they have mutinied, and killed most of the European Officers and civilians. At Merutt and Delhi they have played the mischief, killing not only the European men, but doing so and more to the ladies and children. At Umballa, the European regiments and artillery kept things right, and at Kurnaul and Loodianah there are no troops at present. You will easily find all these places in any good map of India, and they include all the military stations I can recollect at present between Oude and the Punjaub. Now for the Punjaub, in which I am more particularly interested.

On the river Sutledge, which bounds it, are two military stations – Philour and Ferozepore. At the former place there is a Fort manned by a Company of European Infantry and one of Eu. Artillery. The

3rd Native Infantry live outside. Here there has been no row, as the guns of the fort would have polished off the Sepoys quick enough.

At Ferozepore two N. I. regts., the 45th and 57th, mutinied; the 61st European Reg. held the Fort and Magazine, and the artillery and cavalry went out against the mutineers, and all of them who are not killed or in jail have had to throw away their arms and run.

On the road from Philour to Lahore is Jullunder. Here two N. I. and one N. C. regt. mutinied, failed in their attempt to take the artillery guns, and have started off towards Delhi, followed by Europeans and artillery, who, it is hoped, will overtake them. Further up the same road is Umritsar, which is situated just as Philour, viz., the Fort is held by Europeans, and the native troops are helpless.

Next on the river Ravee, are Lahore and Moultan. At both these places the European troops, having the first news of the outbreak, took time by the forelock and disarmed the native troops before they were prepared – 4 regiments at the former, and 2 at the latter place being disarmed, and their lines constantly guarded by European Artillery and Infantry, quietness is the best of their game.

Forty miles north from Lahore you will see Goojeranwalla, where I live. Here, on the first news of the row, the Dy. Commr., ex-Ass. Comm., and myself, who, with their clerk and my overseer, constituted the European residents, raised and armed a lot of the district police, and turned out the 50 men of the 46th N. I., who guarded the treasury, sending them off quietly to their regiment at Sealkot, 30 miles towards the Eastward. We got the Gov. treasure into my house, which, with the garden, we garrisoned, and soon had a force of 300 Infantry and 125 Cavalry, raised and armed from the natives of the district whom we thought we could trust.

At Sealkot the 46th N. I. and half the 9th Cavalry remain still quiet, but we daily expect an outbreak; however, we shall be, I think, right enough here, as they will most likely take the direct route to Umritsar, which does not pass here. Up still further is Jhelum. Here were 2 N. I. regts. – the 39th and 14th, with no Europeans. Before the row was known to the natives there, they sent the 39th off to Dera Ishmail Khan, where a Seikh Regt. will take good enough care of them, but the 14th are daily and hourly expected to rise, in which case they must come this way. We shall try to meet them at Muzerabad with our police, and with the advantage of a river that can only be crossed by boats, and the country people in our favour, I am sanguine that we shall give a good account of them – that is, if they attempt to cross, which I think would be madness for them.

Still higher up is Rawal Pindi, where the 58th N. I. have been disarmed, and are safe enough watched by a European regt. and a Ghoorka regt., which is nearly as good. At Attock there are some Europeans, and with a good fort, quite enough to keep things all right.

At Peshawur and Naushera – for they are so near they may almost be counted as one place – there were 2 European rgts. and 9 of N. I. and 1 of native Cavalry. One, the 55th, rose rather too soon at a place 20 or 30 miles from Peshawur, and thus gave warning to the Europeans, who disarmed all the rest but 2 regts. of N. I., who are supposed to be trustworthy, viz. the 21st and Khelat-i-Ghilzie Regts. Col. Nicholson went at the 55th with his hill regt. of police and some arty. and cavalry, and killed 150, took 100 prisoners, of whom the following day he blew 40 away from guns, and hung the rest, and the remainder of the regt. he hunted into the hills, where they were murdered by the hill tribes; so they have had a lesson of the folly of mutiny. He has also raised large numbers of the hill tribes, who are professional robbers and murderers, and set them to watch the disarmed regts., and at a hint of disturbance they will cut the throats of every man of them.

From this account you will see that in the Punjaub as yet hardly a European life has been lost, and that we have a fair chance of holding our own until European troops come out from England to our assistance. Some few are already dropping in from Madras and Bombay, but, should our attack on Delhi prove a failure, it is to be feared the whole country will rise, and that they will require all their Europeans in their own territories. We hope, and all the well-informed people whom I have seen expect, that 30 or 40 thousand men must ere this have left England to our assistance. We are at present situated thus:– 18 regiments are in open mutiny, and 13 are disarmed, and of the rest of the 10 Cavalry and 74 Infantry regts. of this Presidency, I do not believe *one* will be true if they get a chance to rise.

It is lamentable to think that this should all have come from a foolish attempt of Gen. Anson to interfere with the caste of the men by greasing the bullets of their cartridges with beef suet and pig's fat mixed, and this (although done in ignorance), combined with one or two officers who, with more zeal than prudence, preached to their men, led them to think the Government intended forcibly to make them Christians.

I will write to my mother in a day or two, but do not wish to post more than one letter at once, as a loss of mails is usual enough now. – I am, etc., JOHN CHALMERS

LETTER II

The second paragraph begins with the words 'Below Lucknow'. The word 'below' means lower down the Gangetic plain in the direction of Calcutta and the sea.

Sitapore is about fifty miles north of Lucknow. Aligarh is about a hundred miles south of Delhi. Fategarh lies on the right bank of the Ganges, about a hundred miles north west of Cawnpore (Kanpur).

Hansi is about eighty miles north west of Delhi; Hisar is about fifteen miles to the west of Hansi; Ambala is about sixty miles to the south of the modern city of Chandigarh, towards the foothills of the Himalayas; Karnal is about seventy miles south of Ambala; Ludhiana is about ninety miles to the west of Chandigarh; Philur is a few miles to the north of Ludhiana; Jullundur is about half way between Ludhiana and Amritsar; Multan is about a thousand miles down stream from Lahore.

At this time Chalmers was still a civil engineer with a house of his own, where he seems to have lived for some time, in charge of the work on his section of the trunk road to Peshawar. He writes, however, almost as though he were already a soldier with a detailed knowledge of the military dispositions of British and Indian units covering hundreds of miles of territory in all directions. The letters refer to many more incidents than it is possible for me to describe in this short book, but all of them are narrated in considerable detail in the great work of Sir John Kaye and Col. G. B. Malleson, albeit from standpoints very different from our own.

He describes the promptness and ferocity with which Colonel Nicholson had dealt with mutineers near the frontier. Whatever we may think of such ferocity today, there can be little doubt that the mutiny could have been completely successful, at least in the short run, had such ruthlessness not prevailed over the mutineers, especially in the Punjab.

Whilst Chalmers feels as vengeful as any of his contemporaries, his appreciation of the gross error of the British authorities in attempting to force sepoys to use the greased cartridges reveals his perceptiveness.

LETTER III

GOOJERANWALLA, 22nd June 1857.

My dear Bruce,

It is only a few days since I wrote to you, but although I well know how little interest is generally shown at home in Indian affairs, yet I dare say the recent events may have done something towards exciting people's attention, and you may perhaps like to hear something at first-hand, particularly as the Government, with their usual short-sighted policy, have steadily suppressed the worst, from a foolish fear of what would 'be said in Parliament'. As an instance of this, whilst every one here knows that Delhi is held by 23,000 *mutineers*, who come out daily and give battle to our soldiers, in each of which sorties 400 to 500 are killed, Gov. say in *their* accounts that the *misguided* Sepoys amount to *about* 5000, who are dispirited and without a leader. Yet with fully that number of staunch troops they do not attack, but have ordered 12,000 or 14,000 men to reinforce the army there.

As I have no copy of my last letter, I forget how many regts. were then in arms against the Government, but at present we *know* of 27 in arms and 13 or 14 disarmed, besides which we fear much for the safety of Cawnpore and Allahabad, from which places we have had no news for upwards of a week, and in which there are 3 native regts. each.

I do not think anything could be more disgraceful than the conduct of the Government everywhere, except in the Punjaub where the Lieut.-Gov. took things in his own hands, and pitched all orders from higher powers into the waste-paper basket. Down-country the Mutiny commenced by burning barracks and stations, regts. refusing to take cartridges, and such like nonsense. The Gov. fired proclamations at them, and eventually took the strong measure of, what do you think, to punish two of the most mutinous? – why, paid them up in full, dismissed them from the service, and allowed them to roam about the country to rob and incite other regiments to mutiny. The natural result followed. More than half the army is now in arms against us. Hundreds of Europeans have been murdered in cold blood; European ladies violated, publicly exposed, and then tortured to death. Soldiers have amused themselves by pitching European children about from bayonette to bayonette: in fact, they have tortured and murdered every one they could overpower with a white face, or who, however black, professed Christianity, and this without respect to age or sex. And now, to crown all, the whole country of Rohilcund, the population of which is the most warlike in

India, is in arms against us. Troops are ordered and arriving daily from Madras, Bombay, Ceylon, Pegue, Singapore, the Mauritius, and the Persian Gulf. Steamers are out in all directions to intercept troops *en route* for China, and 30,000 fresh English troops have been applied for from England: in fact, they are now doing on a large scale what they should have done to a moderate extent 3 months ago, and which would have then saved thousands, and I expect before the row is over, hundreds of thousands of lives.

Now for the Punjaub Gov. Here the same sort of thing commenced as below, and, as this was a new and most warlike country, the danger was greater; but fortunately we had men ready to meet it. The Lt.-Gov. burned the proclamations of the Govt., set a most excellent officer, Col. Nicholson (whose life has been spent in border warfare), at the first regt. which broke out (the 55th N. I.), and Col. N., instead of proclamations, paying up, dismissing, etc., went at them with a nice little force of cavalry and arty., killed 150 on the spot, took 100 prisoners, 40 of whom he on the following day blew away from guns in front of the whole frontier army, and most of the others he hanged. The rest of the regt. he hunted into the Levat Hills, when those who consented to become Mohammedans were made so and sold into slavery, one old native officer going so low as 6 pence three farthings, and the others having been *forcibly* made Mohammedans were murdered.

All this sounds cruel, but look to the results of the two systems. That of Hindustan I have told you; but in the Punjaub, although we have had mutineers, we have fought and licked them everywhere. We have disarmed all we could overpower without a serious row, and we overawe the rest with cannon. Not one single European or well-disposed native has been killed as yet, and now, having got things into a pretty fair state, we have spared 1½ European and 3 Punjaubee regiments to the assistance of the lower provinces.

One of the most extraordinary features of the whole business is, that the officers of every reg. without exception believe in their own men, and only awake from their error when they find the muskets pointed at them. The Gov. Gen. has pardoned and reaccepted the services of two native regts. after they had committed themselves; one took the first opportunity of again breaking out, yet he still trusts the other, which will do the same the very first opportunity. The best judges assert that there is *not one* native regt. to be depended upon out of the 74 in the Bengal army list.

You may easily imagine how disgusted I feel that my being a civilian prevents my taking any active part against these scoundrels;

but as engineering is floored for many a day to come, and as volunteer soldiering will not 'keep the pot boiling,' I am amusing myself drilling 200 Seikhs who have been newly raised and of whom I hope to make soldiers. And I have applied to Sir John Lawrence to get me service in the army of some native prince who is still well disposed to us. If I succeed, I may still be at the taking and sack of Delhi – and I can assure you that my vengeance is so excited against the wretches, that I would gladly join in the compact said to be entered into, to give no quarter – With love to all, I am, my dear Bruce, yours sincerely,   JOHN CHALMERS

LETTER III

The 'recent events' to which he refers in the first few lines included some of the most dramatic of the Mutiny. In June alone had occurred the mutiny of the Indian cavalry at Cawnpore (on the 5th), the beginning of the siege of General Sir Hugh Wheeler's earthworks entrenchment at Cawnpore (on the 6th), the outbreak of mutiny at Allahabad (also on the 6th), the massacre at Jhansi (on the 8th) and the outbreak of mutiny at Lucknow (on the 11th).

Whilst Chalmers, as a man very much 'on the spot', expresses understandable impatience with the seemingly slow actions of 'government', both in Calcutta and in London, we should recognize the immense logistic difficulties with which the authorities were faced. The monsoon was about to begin in conditions of great heat, which meant that all troop movements in India would be badly handicapped. And, however urgent the need for reinforcements from overseas, their diversion to India, with the innumerable problems of their feeding and provisioning, and the movements of shipping on a global scale in the early days of the telegraph, must have occupied many weeks. He mentions that troops were arriving daily overland from Bombay and Madras (both little affected by the Mutiny) and by sea from many sources in the East. All such movements must have kept people up for night after night in Whitehall and Calcutta, transcribing telegraphic signals alone, quite apart from dealing administratively with their contents. And what, we may ask, did the miscellaneous commanders in the field and the captains of all the ships feel about the buzzing in their ears?

Chalmers writes: 'The best judges assert that there is *not one* native regiment to be depended upon out of the 74 in the Bengal Army List.' If he was right, the Mutiny was defeated, many months later, by men desperate enough to agree with him. If he was wrong, it was defeated not only by the desperate but by the troops of many Indian regiments whose allegiance to the Company was never lost. That allegiance, however, must be attributed in large measure to the same desperation, which was not exclusively a British experience.

We shall hear more of Colonel Nicholson, who was to lead the mobile column of miscellaneous troops, including many volunteers and former civilian and peasant Indians, and including those raised and trained by John Chalmers. Sir John Lawrence, now Lieutenant-Governor of the Punjab, was responsible for the selection of Nicholson to lead the column against Delhi, and for acceding to Chalmers's request to be granted a commission as an officer in charge of his 'pioneers', as they were first called.

Lord Canning had succeeded Lord Dalhousie as Governor-General at the end of March 1857.

It is interesting that Chalmers should have requested Sir John Lawrence, the virtual ruler of the Punjab, to 'get me service in the army of some native prince who is still well disposed to us'. Despite the ill-treatment of various princes by Dalhousie and by the British government in London, many gave the Company valuable assistance, military and other, during the Mutiny. Chalmers was not affected by the anti-Indian feeling of a great number of his contemporaries who had arrived in India after about 1830.

LETTER IV

GOOJERANWALLA, 23rd June 1857.

My dear Bruce,

Since I wrote to you yesterday there is little news of importance except such as every day brings, viz. of fresh revolts. Cawnpore, I fear, is gone, and if so, a young lady, a sister of a most intimate friend of mine, is in a bad way. She was on her way here from Gloucestershire, and was stopped at Cawnpore on her way.

This morning I got a telegraphic express from Sir John Lawrence appointing me to a new Seikh regiment now on its way to Delhi. It has the start of me about 140 miles, but I hope to overtake it by the day after to-morrow, as I start to-night and take nothing with me but a saddle and bridle, a valaise with two or three shirts, a sword and revolver, and a flask of brandy and a few biscuits. Horses I shall borrow as the one I am on gets knocked up, and ride on so all night and stop in villages all day when it is too hot to travel.

The country through which I pass is pretty quiet, and I expect no interruption. I take no servants or anything except what I mention, except a few shillings to pay for the horses I shall borrow from the villagers, and a bill for £40 to buy me a good horse as soon as I join. My own horses it would be a hopeless thing to try to get down, as the reg. will go as fast as possible, and has already such a start that, even were I to get my horses up, they would be so knocked up as to be worth nothing for some time; but I shall miss my strong, well-tried Punjaubee and Bokhara horses, as I do not like those of Hindoostan much. Again, I am always practising my own for fun at all sorts of work with sword and lance, and the beast I buy will have all to learn. Never mind – that amount should buy me a strong enough brute – beauty I shall not put in the scale at present, and I suspect he will find before I have him an hour that the best of his game will be perfect obedience.

I do not know anything about his regt. I am to join, as Sir John merely says it is a new Seikh levy, and on the road to Delhi. It may be horse, foot, or artillery. However, it is commanded by a very decent fellow whom I know well, and I think it is a Sapper corps. I do not even know whether I am to be 2nd in Command, Adjutant, or Quarter-Master, but I hope and expect the former.

I shall continue my letters as I have opportunity.

I write to my mother to-day, but merely say I am off down-country to another appointment. You can tell her what you please, but if I know her she is not at all likely to fret or feel uneasy. – Love to Helen, and believe me, yours sincerely, JOHN CHALMERS

LETTER IV

Written on the very next day, this letter is one of sudden transformation. Lawrence had given him just what he wanted, again to be a soldier and on his way to smash the mutineers at

Delhi. Even in the midst of war it is only at the rarest moments that such joy can be experienced by a single participant.

We shall never know the wording either of Chalmers's telegram to Sir John Lawrence or of the latter's reply. All we do know is that Lawrence was eager to accept as volunteers able-bodied Europeans and Indians prepared to reinforce the Company's position in those weeks of fear.

The records show that on joining the Bengal Army Chalmers was given the rank of ensign. He was now thirty-six years of age, by which most serving officers had attained much higher rank. He never complained about his rank as such, but various letters not in this collection show that much later in his military service, long after the Mutiny, he was very worried about the level of the pension he could receive after his retirement. The prospect of life in Britain on a very small military pension from the Bengal Army was so forbidding that he thought seriously of remaining in India and attempting to run some kind of business. It seems possible that, when he did retire in 1880 as a major, his second wife, whom he married only in the previous year, was able to contribute something towards their expenses in Paignton in the few years that remained to him.

LETTER V

LOODIANAH, 27th June 1857.

My dear Bruce,

I arrived here during the night before last, and was pretty considerably tired, having come 180 miles in two days and nights – the last 30 of it through a very unsettled country. Indeed, I often wonder how 2 Europeans armed only with sword and pistols could have managed it; but no one interrupted us.

We saw the fine Station of Jullundhur quite deserted – lots of the houses and barracks burned down, and the whole place looking miserable. At Philour we found a force under Gen. Nicholson, of half a European regt., 12 guns with Eu. Arty., and 2 regts. of Native Infantry and half a regt. of Native Cavalry. The previous day Gen. N. had paraded the whole in such a position that the guns ready loaded with grape were turned upon the Sepoys in close column, who were not loaded. He then went up to them and told them that if a man moved or offered to load his musket, the guns would open at once on them. He then ordered them to ground arms, which they had to do at once, and were marched off the ground. At Philour Fort I met lots of old friends – Gulliver of the Engineers, the Commr. of the new corps of Seikh pioneers to which I am attached, Oliphant of the Engineers, under whom I served at Jhelum, and all the officers of the 3rd N. I., whose regt. went away and left them, but did not murder more than one or two. Everything busy in the Fort: new batteries being raised, and ammunition, provisions, etc., arriving in a constant stream; an officer and European sentries constantly on duty, and no native soldier admitted. After a few words with these old friends, who congratulated and envied me on my luck in going to Delhi, I got a glass of brandy and water from one of them to wash some of the dust of my 2 days' and nights' travel out of my throat, and welcome it was as the first thing I had tasted except native bread and very warm and nasty water. N.B. – If you want to know real pleasure, travel so long with the thermometer 135 in the sun and 118 in the shade, and then try a very large tumbler of brandy and iced water. I bet that, like me, you will call for a second.

Gulliver, my C. O., told me that, as he was to halt a day to get arms for the men, I had better come over here to rest and refresh myself, as Mr. Ricketts, the judge, is a friend of mine, and keeps a comfortable bachelor's house. I arrived about 11, found all the Europeans in the place, some 6 or 7, living with Ricketts, and an officer of the 4th Seikh infantry, whom I knew, lying severely wounded by a musket ball, received in trying to prevent the Jullundhur mutineers crossing the river Sutledge.

I got a good bathe, but thought I could never get cleaned from the mud formed of dust and perspiration. However, I did my best, sat down to an excellent breakfast with claret and iced water, quail-pies and everything desirable after two such days as I had passed, and then went to sleep in a well cooled room.

They called me to dinner, and I got up, but went to sleep again immediately afterwards, and this morning find myself *all right* and ready to start for Delhi with my corps.

It is certainly fearful odds we have to contend with, but I think no one who has seen the spirit which animates every European can for a moment doubt the result if troops are speedily sent from England. If not, the case will be a bad one, as let us lick them as we do in every action and kill 400 or 500 of them to our 30 or 40, yet their numbers enable them to afford this loss, and we must be used up in time. Besides, although the Seikhs and Punjaubees are now decidedly with us, would they continue so after one reverse? I fear not.

My host, Mr. Ricketts, did one of the most plucky things here that I ever knew. He found that 3 regts., 2 infty, and 1 cavly., were coming down from Jullundhur to cross the river Sutledge towards this place. He went out to meet this force with 40 men of the 4th Seikhs, a few police, and 2 guns drawn by his own horses.

With this force he opposed them at the river for some hours, killing 50, and obliging them to separate into different parties, and in the end brought off his guns safe, and his small party with a loss of 9, and Lt. Williams severely wounded. Every European shows the same spirit, and *it must succeed*. You cannot imagine how proud I am that the Lt. Gov. should have sent me to Delhi, and that I am the only civilian he has asked. Besides, to take another point of view, in a case of this kind a man is *safer* fighting with an army than living in his own house. We march to-night, and I will write to you from Umballa, where we will arrive in 4 or 5 days.

Give my love to my Mother and Helen and all, and kiss the bairns for me; and believe me, my dear Bruce, yours sincerely,

JOHN CHALMERS

LETTER V

In the first paragraph he shows that he had a European companion (not identified) on his strenuous ride to join his unit at Ludhiana, on the way towards Delhi, in the blazing heat of late June.

The actions of Mr Ricketts, the judge, and Lieutenant Williams are described in detail in Kaye and Malleson's *History of the Indian Mutiny* (vol. 2 pp. 376–80). Nearly all the incidents described by Chalmers are related in their volumes. There is throughout a remarkable coincidence between the two sources.

His reference to the 'old friends' he had met at Philour Fort, though themselves all military officers, must have been encountered during his years as a civilian engineer of the Punjab government service after 1851.

LETTER VI

Camp Punjaub Sappers
Rajpoora, near Umballa,
July 1st, 1857.

My dear Bruce,

I have no news of any kind since I wrote to you from Loodianah, but I now send a few lines merely to let you see how we get on.

We hope if no work detains us on the way, to be before Delhi by the morning of the 8th, but have heard that we have to burn a few villages on the road, the inhabitants of which have stopped the mails and murdered the passengers.

In such a case, all we can do at present is to burn the village and hang the head men, as we cannot spare troops to protect either mails or electric telegraph.

It has been proposed to burn every village within 3 miles of the road, and shoot every man not a soldier or camp follower found within these limits after a certain notice; and this, no doubt, would be effectual, but I hope it will not be ordered until we have got past, as I should not like to be delayed from the grand business, and that hanging and village burning, although a necessary, is but a dirty business at best.

Now that I have seen something of my new corps, I suppose you will expect an account of them. Well, here goes – but it is not flattering.

The Muzbees are the descendants of men of the very lowest caste, who became Seikhs. They are notoriously the *bravest scroundrels* in the country, being in time of war soldiers, but in time of peace usually relaxing their minds by *Thuggee* and *Dacoitee* – two words meaning organised systems of murder and gang robbery. Not a nice lot, you will say, but the main point is that they will fight for pay, and we cannot be nice just now. – Love to all, and believe me, my dear Bruce, yours sincerely,
John Chalmers

I expect my next will be from Delhi.

I enclose an extract from a Lahore newspaper I picked up at Loodianah. I do not know the editor, but shall punch his head on my return. What right has he to speak about a *respectable family*? Your *washerwoman* is, I hope, *respectable*. Otherwise his article is well meant but too late, as Sir John Lawrence was beforehand with him.

LETTER VI

He refers, in his Churchillian English radio manner, to 'Muzbees'. The Sikhs of the Punjab are distinguished, not only by their religion, beards, turbans and codes of conduct, but by a multiplicity of part-ethnic, part-cultural groupings within their own community. Some of them were brought into the community by one or other of the nine successive gurus or spiritual leaders of the community, the last of whom, Govind Singh, had died in the year A.D. 1708. I quote below from a book by Captain R. W. Falcon entitled *Handbook on Sikhs for the Use of Regimental Officers*, published in Allahabad in 1896:

MAZHBI, or Sikh Chuhra, by profession sweepers, some 9% of this very large caste are Sikhs, but the majority cannot be called Mazhbis; the true Mazhbis, or descendants of the family of Chuhrs, admitted to Sikhism by Guru Govind Singh, are not numerous, and it is more than doubtful whether he can supply the required number of recruits for the three Pioneer regiments, and recent Chuhra converts to Sikhism are frequently accepted and enlisted as Mazhbis, the value of the true Mazhbi as a soldier has been proved beyond question, he possesses sterling qualities and though small in build, is wonderfully hard and plucky, admitted as he was by Govind Singh, and specially honoured by the title of Mazhbi or select . . .

In every country the various groupings of the population are more apparent to its inhabitants than to any observers from other parts of the world (however many handbooks may be produced by the latter). Of no country is this more true than India. It is, indeed, the most important fact about the entire subcontinent, and the feature of Indian society which affords its most compelling fascination.

His postscript refers to a report in the *Lahore Chronicle* of 27 June 1857, which, almost by chance, I managed to discover on microfilm. It consists of a long report from Sialkot, about forty miles to the north east of Gujranwalla, dated the 22nd:

. . . I believe some 5 or 600 Sikhs have been lately raised at Goojranwalla, under the auspices of Mr Cripps, the Deputy Commissioner, and I am told greatly assisted by Mr Jno (*sic*) Chalmers, the Assistant Civil Engineer. Mr Chalmers is an old brave soldier, formerly belonging to the corps of Sappers, a man of respectable family, and of sound education, why not give him the command of that corps to be trained and disciplined by him – he knows the Sikhs and their language well. That we have not sufficient Commissioned Officers and European soldiers to meet the pressing danger is apparent . . .

Chalmers's pugilistic comment is a little odd. Did he feel patronized? Or was a punch on the head no more than a figurative friendly greeting whilst glasses are raised in a pub? The passage of time locks away little keys to understanding.

LETTER VII

KURNAUL, 5th July 1857.

My dear Bruce,

I wrote to you the other day from Rajpoora, and posted the letter at Umballa, and you will see by a look at the map that we are getting on towards Delhi at the rate of 20 to 25 miles a night, which is double the usual marches even in cold weather, whilst this is fearfully hot, and we do not wait for tents or anything.

Although there had been a severe action at Loodianah with the mutineers, who lost 58, whilst our men lost some 15, with a European officer severely wounded and a native officer killed, yet the storm had passed, and the country was pretty quiet, and the only signs of it I saw were the skeletons, and the remains of red jackets I noticed near the roadside.

From there we have found the road clear so far, but in Umballa the church, which is the largest in India, has been strongly fortified and turned into an hospital for the wounded. I went with the engineer to see it, and I can assure you the effect was something new. The yard was surrounded with a ditch and strong earthen rampart with bastions at the corners, mounted with heavy 24 lb. guns, and the gateways defended by 18 and 12 pounders. The windows were all built up and crenelled for musketry, whilst the church itself was filled with beds for the sick and provisions for some months, in case of a siege.

To-day 140 of the most severely wounded men of our army were brought in here on their way to Umballa, and all night we heard heavy firing, although Delhi is 70 miles off. We start to-night, and expect to have to fight our way in, the last day, unless they can spare guns and cavalry to escort us in. We shall reach, if all is right, in 4 days.

The wounded officers tell us that all along we have only been able to *hold our own against the attacks* of the enemy, and that we have done nothing against the city, and cannot, until large reinforcements arrive. This we hardly suspected to be so bad, as the Govt. publish flourishing accounts, and private are stopped as much as possible, so it may be some time before I can write another to you, but I shall lose no opportunity.

In one attack of the enemy on the 23rd ult. our troops were so hard pressed that the officers were going to spike and abandon the guns, but a Seikh regt. came up, having marched 30 miles in the sun that day, and turned the scale to our favour most gallantly.

Indeed the Punjaub altogether has afforded a strong contrast to the imbecility shown elsewhere, and if India is saved, Sir John Lawrence has done it, and should be made a Duke.

Love to Mother, Helen, and all; and believe me, my dear Bruce, your aff. Brother, JOHN CHALMERS

Our men, although recruits, are in fine spirits, and we have not had one desertion in spite of the killing marches we have made.

LETTER VI

For the historian this letter is one of the most challenging. First, it brings home to us the enormous energy and determination that was required of officers and men if the mutineers were to be defeated, as they must. The long exhausting marches of the various columns converging upon Delhi had to be undertaken during the early part of the monsoon. They marched at night to avoid the intense heat and saturated atmosphere of the daylight hours, but when the soil must have been heavy with mud and the air singing wiith the piercing sound of mosquitoes, which attack at night. Most of the troops were Indians of the Punjab, including many Sikhs, and the loyalty of those columns, whether on the march or in battle, was phenomenal.

Second, we have Chalmers's contrast between the effective authority of Sir John Lawrence and the 'imbecility shown elsewhere'. Elsewhere meant, to such observers as Chalmers, Calcutta and the government of Lord Canning. This contrast demands analysis. Sir John (1811–79), whilst possessing the instinct of a soldier, was throughout a civilian administrator. He had been Chief Commissioner of the Punjab since 1852. I quote the following passages from the long account of his career in the *Dictionary of National Biography*:

By the month of August, 1857... the tide had turned in Bengal, and with the fall of Delhi the ultimate suppression of the Mutiny became certain. To none more than to Sir John Lawrence does the credit for this issue belong.

Largely cut off from Calcutta by the events of the Mutiny to the East, Sir John had taken military responsibilities on his own, including the mobilization of the various columns, including the 'irregular Sikhs' of Chalmers's own unit, for the recapture of Delhi. He had dealt with the mutiny in the whole North West by extremely prompt decisions, preempting mutinous outbreaks by forcibly disarming troops, hanging ring-leaders or seeing that effective attacks were made against any actual mutineers. He made himself feared, but respected for his merciful decisions at the same time.

Early in 1859 he was threatened with congestion of the brain and racked by neuralgia, and he found himself half blind. His doctors feared an attack of paralysis. On 28 February 1859 he handed over the government of the Punjab to Montgomery, and, travelling by the Indus and Kurrachi to Bombay, reached England after an absence of seventeen years. His services had been rewarded in October with the Grand Cross of the Bath and in the spring and autumn of 1858 (in absentia) he received the freedom of the City of London and was sworn of the Privy Council.

He was appointed Viceroy on 30 November 1863, 'in ten days he was on his way to Calcutta'. He ruled India with great personal authority till 12 January 1869. On his retirement he was created Baron Lawrence of the Punjab and of Grateley, a small village in Hampshire where there was a little family property. His years as viceroy were distinguished by major contributions to the economic infrastructure of the country, including substantial extensions of the railway system, trunk roads and long canals. The canals, though useful as means of transport, were even more of an asset in facilitating the irrigation of wide stretches of the Northern plains, thus providing food for the ever-expanding population of the future down to our own day. The railways proved invaluable, especially in times of drought or failure of the monsoon, for the relief of famines. Lawrence was probably the most important British figure of the century in India.

What can we make of the 'imbecility' of Lord Canning, the Governor-General of the Mutiny period, in Calcutta? It seems likely that, residing well over a thousand miles away from the North West Frontier zone, from which the gravest dangers to British authority were apprehended by Lawrence and his able colleagues, Canning *felt* the sense of urgency somewhat less acutely than they did. However that may be, Canning showed wisdom and humanity in his decisions about the part to be played by retribution in the treatment of defeated or captured mutineers, or about what should be done with those who had been disarmed. Here is a short passage from *The Competition Wallah* (1864 edition) by Sir George Otto Trevelyan, first published in 1862, in which, in the form of imaginary letters, he discusses the recent mutiny and its aftermath.

The wise ruler, whose comprehensive and impartial judgment preserved him from the contagion of that fatal frenzy, was assailed with a storm of obloquy for which we should in vain seek a precedent in history. To read the newspapers of that day, you would believe that Lord Canning was at the bottom of the whole mutiny; that upon his head was the guilt of the horrors of Cawnpore and Allahabad; that it was he who had passed round the chupatties and the lotahs, and spread the report that the Russ was marching down from the North to drive the English into the sea. After all, the crime charged against him was, not that he had hindered the butchery, but that his heart was not in the work. No one had the face to say, or, at any rate, no one had the weakness to believe, that Lord Canning had pardoned any considerable number of condemned rebels. His crying sin was this, that he took little or no pleasure in the extermination of the people whom he had been commissioned by his Sovereign to govern and protect.

LETTER VIII

Camp before Delhi,
10th July 1857.

My dear Bruce,

I arrived here yesterday about 10 o'clock in the morning, after marching all night since 5 the previous afternoon. We had charge of some 150 carts and 200 camels, and consequently the rear-guard, which I commanded, was some 1½ or 2 miles behind the advance.

After the advance-guard had got into camp a party of mutineers, infantry and cavalry, came out from the city, got *round* our camp unobserved, and attacked my convoy.

The drivers bolted like fun, with the camels and bullocks. I with my party pushed on, and, passing the carts loaded with articles of comparatively small value, got up to those containing ammunition, which I protected. My men, although marched off their legs and all recruits, stood well, and showed no sign of bolting. We were not attacked at close quarters, as a large force came out of camp to our support, and gave battle to the mutineers.

I had a sergeant who was in charge of the stores killed but no one else even touched. In the engagement that ensued the mutineers are said to have lost 500 killed, besides wounded, but I do not believe it, as no one that I have seen has *himself* counted more than 196 dead bodies, and I do not believe in their having had time to carry in their dead.

We lost 50 killed and about 100 wounded, so that altogether it was a sharp beginning to my service.

By afternoon I got my carts and camels collected, and brought into camp – every one – and found my way to the Sapper mess-house, where I find 20 Engineers live in one room, dining off an old billiard-table that escaped destruction, and the edges of which they have cut off. At night some sleep on the table, and some in the verandah.

Up to date we *know* of 37 regts. in mutiny, and 16 disarmed, out of the 74.

Things here are much worse than my worst fears, and should *very strong* reinforcements not arrive soon, good-bye to English rule in India; but I will write all about it as soon as I have seen for myself – that is, if one of these shells – that *will* burst near our house – does not prevent me.

Love to Mother and Helen, and believe me, yours sincerely,

John Chalmers

LETTER VIII

In Kaye and Malleson's history (vol. II) there is a large-scale map showing the dispositions of the Company's troops before Delhi about half a mile to the north of the walled circumference of the city and a similar distance to the west of the Jumna river. The walls of the city must not be confused with the towering walls of the Moghul palace, or Red Fort, within the city and adjoining the river. The lines of the Sappers and Miners, with whom Chalmers was presumably stationed with his Sikhs, were a few hundred yards to the west of the other troops.

Chalmers's description of casualties incurred during the fighting on the hard approach march seems to our minds laconic, but no participant in a war who manages to survive can do so unless he develops a detachment of that kind. It can neither be anticipated in advance nor retrieved in retrospect.

His penultimate paragraph expresses a gloomy view of the position. He was a man of fast bodily metabolism, moods of enthusiasm and of depression alternating in rapid succession with fatigue and recuperation.

His letters do not seem to have been subjected to any system of censorship comparable with that associated with modern war, during which attempts are made to delete from a man's letters passages which appear to be conducive to the spread of 'despondency' among readers on the 'home front'. Such a notion as the 'home front' had not entered the consciousness of the nineteenth century.

LETTER IX

CAMP DELHI, 11th Aug. 1857.

My dear Bruce,

On coming in from a hard night's work in the batteries, I have just heard that a mail starts to-day, so I, although very tired and sleepy, write a few lines that you and my Mother and sisters may know I am still all right.

We are still holding on here waiting for reinforcements, having every 2nd or 3rd day to fight some 10 or 12 times our number of the mutineers, whom we regularly lick. We have had in all some 30 engagements, and although *always* successful, yet the inevitable loss reduces our *little* force surely, if gradually. Will it be believed, that in weather when it was always considered impossible for Europeans to go outside, 3000 or less have here for two months held their own against 40,000 or 50,000 natives, equally well armed and drilled, and superior in artillery and every necessary of war.

We anxiously wait for reinforcements from Calcutta, from which direction we can get no certain information, but report says Lucknow and Cawnpore are as bad as, or worse off than, ourselves, and that *all Europeans* at the latter place are murdered. The Lahore route is the only one open now. – Love to all, and believe me, your aff. brother,

JOHN CHALMERS

Address:
ENS. CHALMERS Adj. P. S. & M.,

LETTER IX

A whole month had elapsed since the last letter was written.

He refers to 'a hard night's work in the batteries'. The commander of the forces before Delhi was now Brigadier Archdale Wilson, an artillery officer, and his adviser on engineering questions was Major Baird Smith, Chief Engineer. The British position was extremely difficult at this stage. The various columns, including that which had included Chalmers himself, as they converged upon the city, expecting to go into an attack, had been halted by innumerable powerful sorties of mutineers from the city, of the kind described in the previous letter. This had caused Wilson to consider a withdrawal until much greater reinforcements from the Punjab could arrive. The month had been spent on the defensive, the would-be besiegers of the city having become the besieged, among whom casualties could ill be afforded.

The Chief Engineer had advised strongly against any such withdrawal. The strength of the mutineers in the city was constantly growing, their reinforcements trickling in daily from other parts of the country, including, of course, Jhansi. Such reinforcements considerably outweighed the hundreds of mutineers who were killed whenever they ran into the approaching British forces. A British withdrawal would have enabled the mutineers in the city to move widely over Northern India, to the detriment of the Company's position generally.

Baird Smith advised Wilson to hold fast, and to utilize the time required for more reinforcements to arrive, for the purpose of building the strongest possible gun emplacements, close to the city walls, in preparation for the necessary breach to come. Wilson accepted that advice, which explains the nightly tasks of sapper officers like John Chalmers.

Note the address at the foot of the letter, which means: Ensign Chalmers, Adjutant, Pioneers, Sappers and Miners. The address at Lahore implies that letters were sorted there. As modern soldiers know well, as their units approach a battlefield, their personal letters have to be addressed to some base to the rear, whence they are forwarded by whatever means can be found on any day.

LETTER X

CAMP BEFORE DELHI,
28th Aug. 1857.

My dear Bruce,

I now take up my pen to let you know how things are going on here, and as this is an extra mail and we are only allowed a limited amount of weight each, I must write as close as I can.

I came down here in an indefinite sort of position, attached to a corps of 300 Punjaub Sappers, and on my first arrival had lots of work with them. Raids into the enemy's country for timber and stores; reducing refractory villages and hanging their head men, and shooting all we could find armed; varied by nights in the trenches and batteries, where we had to work night after night at the same time that we afforded pleasant amusement to the enemy, who usually kept up a steady fire of grape, canister, and musketry on us; but now that my corps is increased to 700 bayonettes, and men are on the way down and daily expected, to raise it to 1100, I am struck off all duty – appointed by the C. in C. Ensign and Adjutant, and labour from morning till night teaching stupid recruits and larky young officers the mysteries of the goose-step and how to shoot. Well, if I am not quite so pleasantly, I am fully as usefully employed, and I suppose that when the storm takes place I will find some way of getting into it or other.

We now number about 9000 men here, of whom 4000 are European soldiers, and the rest Punjaub recruits, and with these, please God, we will take Delhi in a few days, garrisoned as it is by

24,000 regular and first-rate troops, and any number of well-armed blackguards – or expend ourselves in the attempt.

The day before yesterday we got the Home News, and I can hardly say whether indignation, disgust, or a sense of the ludicrous prevailed when we found that England was to send out round the Cape, and consequently to arrive in 6 or 7 months, 3000 men to quell a mutiny of 80 or 90 thousand well-armed and disciplined troops, who have a whole country with them, and who have already murdered every man, and done far worse to every woman bearing the name of Briton, who lived out of Calcutta, the Punjaub, or the one or two stations where there were considerable bodies of European troops; and then the papers wind up with a lot of bombast, alluding, I suppose, to the 3000, who by the time they reach the scene of action will be reduced by sickness to 800 or 900, about what a mighty empire does to assert its injured majesty!

Well, here we are cut off from all communication with any place below Agra, with information that we are to get no assistance from Calcutta, and with the Punjaub still staunch, but of course doubtful, but for all this with good hearts, and a full intention of doing our duty and taking Delhi.

The day before yesterday the enemy sent out 6 regiments of infantry with a lot of cavalry and guns to our rear, when one of our Punjaub men, Gen. Nicholson, went after them with a small party, licked them, took all their camp equipage and 13 guns, and killed a lot, but unfortunately was not strong enough to prevent the return to the city of most of them. This is where our want of numbers tells.

I shall constantly write a few lines every mail to let you know how we get on.

Give my love to all, and believe me, my dear Bruce, your aff. brother, JOHN CHALMERS

I enclose a line or two to Mother, but really can say little that would interest her.

LETTER XI

CAMP BEFORE DELHI,
28th Aug. 1857.

My dearest Mother,

I have just heard that a mail starts to-day, and so sit down to write you a few lines, from which you will see that we are still on the outside of this accursed city.

Our force is small, but with reinforcements we have lately had from the Punjaub we hope to try it soon, fearful as the odds against us are; and although I am now as adjutant struck off all work in the trenches, and everything except the drill and discipline of my corps, I hope to manage so as to be one of the first inside.

The weather is very hot to live in tents, and lots of our friends go off daily from wounds and sickness, but I am very well, and although I hope I have done my duty, untouched in any way.

As we are only allowed two letters each by this, which is an extra post, and you will see Bruce's, I send you very few lines, but I know you value them in proportion to the affection that dictates them and not by quantity. – I am, my dear Mother, your very aff. son,

JOHN CHALMERS
Ensign and Adjt., Punjaub Pioneers

LETTER XII

CAMP BEFORE DELHI,
15th Sept. 1857.

My dear Bruce,

I have only time for a line to say that at length we have walked over the walls of Delhi, and during yesterday have taken about one-third of the city, the fighting being still going on by reliefs of men who come back to camp to rest.

I suppose you will be anxious to know how it feels to attack a breach in a wall. Well, all I can say is that those who are killed know nothing about it. Those who are not, perhaps do not like it; but for those who, like me, escape, it is rather a pleasant excitement, and I think on the whole superior to hunting.

First, although you see lots fall about you, somehow it never occurs to you that your hour may come. Then, what with looking after and keeping your men together, you have no time to *funk*. Our loss has been *awfully* severe, Gen. Nicholson amongst the rest, and the only man here we could depend upon to lead.

I do not yet know how things may turn out with us, but the taking of Delhi must at any rate dishearten the rebels and cut them off from supplies. Will England not send us assistance instead of talking in Parliament?

I have before me a list of 240 *commissioned officers known* to have been murdered; and when the clerks, sergeants, privates, poor European civilians, and all the wives and families, not to speak of the numbers killed in fair fighting, are added to this, the list will, I think, open people's eyes in England.

Just as we got into the city we found the body of a European chained to a stake and *roasted* – not burned – to death. I don't think the sight was for the good of the natives who fell into our hands. – I am, my dear Bruce, your aff. brother, JOHN CHALMERS

LETTER XIII

CAMP DELHI, 15th September [1857].

My dear Mother,

As there is a *chance* still of a letter going by this mail, I write a few lines in hopes it may reach you. Since the 7th I have not had a moment that I could spend in that way, and even had I the time the means were wanting.

On the evening of the 7th, after having been warned to go with my men to construct advanced batteries, I wrote a few lines which I sealed and addressed to you in case I should have been knocked over, but as that did not occur I shall destroy it as soon as I get my traps collected and find the key of my desk.

Well, on the night of the 7th, my corps erected the first advanced battery, and, having worked all night under a very heavy fire of round-shot, grape, and musketry which floored many a good man, we got it finished and 10 guns at work at the city by daybreak.

From then to Sunday night I lived, or rather existed, in a constant state of hard work, with the additional excitement of shot and shell.

On Sunday night I came home to my tent and went to bed, in the confidence that I was to have a good night's sleep. At 3 I was awoke by an orderly with a letter telling me that I was to start immediately with 100 picked men of my corps to join the assault, and that the rest were to follow with the other officers. I did so, got safe in over the breach, and fought and worked all day in the heat until 6 at night when I was relieved and sent home to rest.

By that time one-third of the city was our own, and the fighting still continues, and, from the immense extent of the city and the obstinacy with which every inch is contested, it will probably be 3 or 4 days before we have it all.

The less I say about the whole affair the better, as it could not be a pleasant subject to you, although to me, who had many dear and kind friends to revenge, it was so. I got off without a scratch, although my clothes were shot in more than one place; but I believe I did, and was acknowledged to have done, my duty. My escape can be only considered as a most extraordinary one, as out of 14 engineers employed during the day, 10 were either killed or wounded, whilst I was there from the first until 6 at night.

With love to all, believe me, my dear Mother, your aff. son,

JOHN CHALMERS

LETTER XII & XIII

The assault upon Delhi began on 14 September and the last strongholds of the mutineers in the city were captured on the 20th.

Brigadier-General Sir John Nicholson, the immensely strong, intrepid character of the North West, was fatally wounded in the assault and died on the 22nd, living just long enough to be aware of the victory. He had organized and led the famous Movable Column, available to crush outbreaks of mutiny wherever they might occur in North Western India.

Having regard to what Chalmers wrote to his mother in Letter XIII, the capture of Delhi had been throughout very largely founded upon the work of the sappers.

LETTER XIV

CAWNPORE, 8th February 1858.

My dear Mother,

About a fortnight ago I wrote a letter to Bruce from Futtygurh, and had commenced one to you, when we got sudden orders to march for Cawnpore and Lucknow, and I had to lay my paper by and get the men ready.

Yesterday we arrived here, and to-morrow we go on, but as we are to be allowed only one tent per regiment and one servant each, I have so much to do making arrangements for the things we do leave behind, that I can only send you a very short letter.

I do not know whether it is the excitement of again getting something to do, or what, but I am now as well as ever I was, and I only hope that when the Lucknow affair is over I may not pay too heavy a price for the exposure and excitement. I always wished to be at the settling it off.

We go at it under very different circumstances from Delhi, as we expect to have 20,000 men and no end of guns, whereas in Delhi, although at the last we had nominally 10,000, so many were sick and wounded that we could never muster 5000.

I went yesterday, after I came in, to see the house where the women and children were killed and the well into which they were thrown. The former is all knocked down, as it was in the way of the new fortifications, so I only saw the ruins. The latter is filled up, built over, and a neat little monument erected. I also went to see

Gen. Wheeler's entrenchment – it is no shelter whatever; I rode over it on my old horse with ease, and could only wonder how it was held so long. I, like every one else, I believe, came away from these sights with feelings of revenge I never felt before.

As I will most probably have no chance of sending a letter for some time – not at least until Lucknow is altogether ours – I hope you will not be uneasy. The same Providence that guided me through the long, and tedious, and dangerous siege, and bloody assault of Delhi, where more than a third of our people were knocked over, can still protect me through the comparatively easy affair we have now to meet. And consider that a *civilian*, as I have so long been, who goes through both, will be a sort of curiosity afterwards.

I am now very ill-mounted, as this work is murder to horseflesh, and I went out yesterday to try to buy. The only thing I saw at all like my weight was an Arab at the moderate price of £200. Before this row I could easily have bought him for £50. I could not make up my mind to pay such a price, so I go on with my old one, and will take my chance of *finding* one in Lucknow.

By the bye, I see the Government have become ashamed of themselves and are going to give us the Delhi prize-money after all, but they have so fearfully mismanaged it that my share will be barely £200. I hope better from Lucknow.

Give my love to the girls and their children, and best respects to John Mackenzie and Bruce; and believe me, my dear Mother, your ever aff. JOHN

LETTER XIV

Five months have elapsed since the last letter in this collection. He probably sent other letters during that period, but if so they were not among the bundle found in his mother's house at Wishaw.

The capture of Delhi had greatly strengthened the British position, by releasing forces, including Chalmers's sappers, that were now able to join the other columns slowly converging (from Bombay, Calcutta and Delhi), upon the two cities of Lucknow and Cawnpore to the south. Such movements during the monsoon must have been difficult to plan and exhausting for all the troops involved. The slow pace of movement and the ceaseless problems of all officers, and especially those with the duties of adjutants, would have left him with little leisure for writing letters. By 8 February, however, the fresh, dry weather had brought the annual season of warfare back into daily imminence. His reference to 'one tent per regiment' shows that the time had come when, with the aid of a blanket only, most troops would have slept beneath the stars, free of insects at last.

The story of Wheeler's entrenchment and the events at Cawnpore is described briefly in pp. 78–85 above.

LETTER XV

CAMP BEFORE LUCKNOW,
13th February 1858.

My dear Bruce,

I wrote to you from Futtygurh and to my Mother from Cawnpore, and to-day I got your letter of the 24th December enclosed in one of hers.

You send also a note of the troops that have come out. We have already the *immense number* of 4000 collected here, but we hope before the time the weather sets in hot enough to finish off all the fresh ones, to have 20,000 collected, and to be able to assault the place with some hopes of fairly polishing it off, and not, as was done at Delhi, fighting our way in at one end with some 3000 effective men, and allowing all the enemy to escape at the other end.

The fact is, my dear fellow, that months have been wasted – first, by sending the men out in sailing-vessels instead of steamers; again, by the want of arrangement in Calcutta for sending them up the country; and last, but not least, by the *funk* that induced the big-wigs in Calcutta to keep every man they could as long as they possibly could for the protection of their precious persons against nothing.

The consequence is, that although Sir Colin got this length once before, and relieved the garrison so far as to take away the women and sick, and also to leave them some assistance and provisions, he was unable either to keep the road open in his rear, or to relieve 8 unfortunate Europeans in the city, 4 of whom were blown away from guns the day he left. The enemy had closed on his rear in the meantime, and on his return to Cawnpore he found Gen. Wyndham well licked and shut up in the entrenchment, and he, Sir Colin, had to attack the enemy, and, having thrashed them, follow them to Futtygurh and drive them over the river.

When there, he had not men for anything effectual; he certainly put the fort in order, and, after waiting there 3 weeks for ammunition from Agra and Delhi, most of which had come down from the Punjaub, he is now on his way here to besiege Lucknow, just as the weather is getting fearfully hot, and, after all, he will not have more than 20,000 men, of whom 5000 or 6000 have come down from the Punjaub, to attack a large and strong town, garrisoned by 30,000 regular troops, 600 guns, and no end of well-armed blackguards. However, we mean to take it, – we will, and that before long. As for us, we are by this time pretty well climate-proof, but the new arrivals will suffer terribly.

Sir Colin is, they say, in good spirits, but thinks he is ill-used in their not sending troops up from Calcutta. Sir John Lawrence has got up a plan of getting them from Bombay to Lahore, and then here, and, although the distance is double, he expects to beat the Calcutta people in speed. He only started it the other day so I cannot say how it will do.

I will write again as soon as we do anything. – Love to Helen and the young ones, and believe me, yours sincerely,   JOHN CHALMERS.

This reminds me of Delhi, guns going all day and all night too, but the enemy's batteries are at so prudent a distance that they hurt no one, and we do not even reply.

LETTER XV

As in some of the letters written before the assault upon Delhi, Chalmers expresses pessimism and a bitter humour. His complaint about sending British reinforcements in sailing ships instead of in steamers is understandable, but we have no reason to believe that he had any knowledge of the availability of the latter. Another factor could have vexed him even more had he known of it. In October the Emperor of the French, Napoleon III, in a gesture of friendship for Britain, offered to allow British troops to travel across France by train to Toulon on their way to India, thus saving the long voyage from Southampton via Gibraltar and the Western Mediterranean. The result was a snub from Palmerston, the British Prime Minister. The following account of the background is of interest:[*]

It was essential for Louis Napoleon's policy to maintain good

---

[*]Jasper Ridley, *Napoleon III and Eugénie*, London, 1979, pp. 419–20.

relations with Britain; but public opinion in both Britain and France made this difficult. When news of the rebels' successes in the Indian Mutiny reached London and Paris in October 1857, Louis Napoleon made a gesture of sympathy with Britain by offering to allow British reinforcements to travel through France and embark at Toulon in order to shorten the time taken for their six weeks' journey to Bombay. But Palmerston declined the offer, and greatly resented what he interpreted as an attempt by Louis Napoleon to make the world believe that Britain could not suppress the mutiny without his help. With more reason, the British were alarmed at the large scale naval building programme on which Louis Napoleon had embarked in 1857, though the French pointed out that even when the programme was completed, Britain would still have naval superiority over France.

By September news had reached London of the atrocities committed by the Sepoy mutineers against British women and children at Cawnpore and elsewhere, and the British press were publishing editorials demanding vengeance on the whole Indian people and letters from British officers boasting of how they had hanged and burned wholesale in Indian villages and massacred unarmed civilians in the capture of Delhi. This was too good an opportunity for the French press to miss. For years they had been lectured by *The Times* and other English newspapers on the cruelties of the French in Algeria and the wickedness of Louis Napoleon's despotism in France; and they now gave great publicity to the decree of the Governor-General of India suppressing all native-language newspapers, and to the most hysterical of the demands for hangings and floggings that were published in *The Times*, *The Morning Post* and *The Bombay Times*.

During periods of atrocity, we criticize the conduct of others. In retrospect we criticize ourselves. Responding to British opinion, Palmerston made the wrong decision.

The 'camp before Lucknow' was the principal assembly point for the various columns that were being assembled for the re-taking of the city, now devoid of British forces and left in the hands of the mutineers. It was located in the grounds of the Alum Bagh, about a mile and a half to the south of the city, in a somewhat isolated position. It is described by Colonel Malleson thus:

... a garden in the suburbs of Lucknow, literally 'The Garden of the World' within an enclosure of 500 square yards. There is a building within the garden, containing many rooms in the second story. The Alum Bagh was built by the last King of Oudh, Wajid Ali, as an occasional residence for a favourite wife. Within the garden is Sir Henry Havelock's tomb, surmounted by an obelisk with an inscription written by his widow. The place commands the road from Lucknow to Cawnpore.*

The word 'bagh' is of interest. It cannot be translated exactly into English. Broadly, it usually means the residence of some important personage, including a house, mansion or palace and the grounds in which it is situated, the whole often surrounded by walls, more or less of a defensive nature. It corresponds roughly with a traditional manor house in Britain, with a similar historical origin. In and about Lucknow there were many 'baghs' and the term is widely used in the Indian subcontinent. At Patna, for example, the official residence of the Chief Justice of Bihar (who was my father) was called Chhajju Bagh, and is now the residence of the Indian Chief Justice. The surrounding wall of the estate is considerable, and the area now contains many buildings apart from the residences of the Chief Justice and other members of the judiciary of the state of Bihar.

I cannot, within the scope of this book, adequately summarize all the military movements mentioned in the letters. Chalmers refers incorrectly to Major-General Charles A. Windham, CB. Sir Colin Campbell, in the action mentioned in this letter, although he had inflicted a heavy blow upon the mutineers in Lucknow by killing about two thousand of them in savage fighting, before rescuing all the British personnel, military and civilian, from the ruins of the Residency and taking them to Cawnpore, felt obliged to abandon Lucknow and return to Cawnpore to assist Windham, who had too few troops to hold his position there. He returned for the final conquest of Lucknow three weeks later. By that time the women and children had been moved on to safety at Allahabad and Calcutta.

*Kaye and Malleson, *History of the Indian Mutiny*, vol.IV, 1889, p. xiii.

LETTER XVI

CAMP BEFORE LUCKNOW,
13th February 1858.

My dear Mother,

Your very welcome letter of the 24th December, enclosing one from Bruce, I have just received. As I only arrived here yesterday, you were rather premature in addressing to Lucknow, but to your doing so, I suspect, I owe the receipt of the letters. What put it into your head that I was here? for when your letter was written I had not the least idea myself that I had a chance of coming down.

We are encamped to the rear of Allumbagh (the Garden of Allum), and have sent out working parties to-day to prepare materials for the siege. We are in an open plain, and the enemy have surrounded us with batteries from which they keep up lots of noise, but they have constructed them at so prudent a distance that they do us little or no harm.

We have some 4000 men here in all, but, to judge by what we saw on the road, we should have 20,000 and lots of guns shortly. I only hope they will let us into the place quickly, as the weather begins to get hot, and if we wait about outside we may expect half the men who are fresh from England to die off. They say the place is very strong. I have not had a look at it yet, as my old horse has had constant work for some time and has got a sore back. I therefore give him a rest to-day, but to-morrow I must go and have a look at the city walls from as near a point as may be prudent.

I am glad you saw some notice of my name in the papers. I had not done so myself, and thought it hardly fair, as I honestly think I did as much as my neighbours. Had Nicholson lived I think he would have mentioned it. Our men, I also think, got scarcely the notice they deserved, but it is generally so with irregular troops. Gen. Chamberlain said in his report to Sir John Lawrence that their courage amounted, in his opinion, to utter recklessness of life, and I was glad of that, as I have always been in front of them wherever they have gone.

I know who Mrs Dewis is: her husband was a sergeant under Major Maxwell and made lots of money, but I did not know, although I may have met him. He would no doubt know my name well.

I shall try to find out Graham Lockhart, but as you do not mention his regiment I may not succeed. You, or Bruce, mentioned some Doctor he knew-here, but I never keep letters now, on the chance of their falling into other hands, and I have lost the memorandum I made of his name. I think he belonged to the 3rd Bat. of Rifles.

I know there were some *small* rows in some of the Bombay regs., but they were kept very quiet. I did not, however, hear that it had gone the length of people running for their lives.

Did you see Harley Maxwell? You mention him in your letter. I met him some 2½ years ago at a wedding, and breakfasted with him next morning.

I hope yet to see you all again, but am not at all sanguine about it. I have indeed a lot to tell – would a book pay? – 'Nine years' residence in India, with twelve months in Cashmere and the hills, and a turn at almost everything going during the Rebellion of '57 and '58.'

I do not know whether they will give me a permanent commission or not. I fear my health will not suit it long, but will try. I am now about as well off as I was before the row took place, or rather better – that is to say, I may be worth £500 or £600. If I could get it up to £1500, I would be inclined to try some business out here, such as a paper mill, a distillery, or a farm, either of which would pay far better than Government employment does for an honest man here. We will see if Lucknow gives us any prize-money. Delhi will be very little. Indeed, it has been so fearfully mis-managed, some Bombay people, who had only half an hour's fighting altogether, share for Ensigns £905 each, whilst, as yet, for my 6 months I have not £200 or anything like it. – With love to all, I am, my dear Mother, your aff. son,

JOHN CHALMERS

LETTER XVII

CAMP NEAR LUCKNOW,
22nd February 1858.

My dear Bruce,

My Mother's letter of the 16th Jany., enclosing one from you, I received yesterday, being 1 month and 4 days, besides having gone round by Agra. It is the quickest I have ever had, and shows that the roads are pretty open and safe.

When I wrote to you a few days ago I think I said that we hoped to go in at Lucknow with 20,000 men before the hot weather. Alas, I was disappointed, as Sir Colin has had to return to Cawnpore to keep the communications open after almost reaching us, and now it is the Delhi affair over again but rather worse.

Our position is about this. We, about 5000 strong of all arms, are sitting down in front of a city defended by at the very least 100,000 men, armed and drilled, and most of whom are, or were at some former time, Sepoys of our own. This city we say we are attacking, whereas the fact is that we are almost daily attacked ourselves, and have to spend all the time not taken up in the repulse of the attacks in fortifying our position. We can do nothing against the city, which is getting stronger every day. Since Sir Colin relieved the Residency and got every one out, it is known that the enemy have dug a ditch 40 feet wide and 30 deep, round, at any rate, a considerable part of the town. With the assistance of the Punjaub and the Delhi force, Sir Colin can muster somewhere about 19,000 or 20,000 men of all ranks and colours, of which it seems 15,000 are barely enough to keep open the communications in our rear, leaving us about 5000 men under Gen. Outram — and the hot weather fairly set in. I dined with Gen. O. the day before yesterday. He of course says little about it, but he seems to feel the delay of troops as much as any of us.

Yesterday (Sunday) we had a grand attack upon our camp, and I was out all day with our men. Of course the rebels were beaten back, but their constant attacks are tiresome.

Now I know you must think me a croaker, but my opinion is the same now as it was at first, viz. that every day this affair is allowed to go on makes it worse. What 5000 men could have done in May in Delhi with ease, 10,000 hardly succeeded in, in September, and 20,000 could scarcely do now in Lucknow, and if the row lasts much longer 50,000 will not do in 6 months' time. In India a row is like a snowball. In May the mutineers in Delhi were 6000 or 7000, in September something like 50,000, and now in Lucknow they are 100,000, rendered cautious by defeat, and increasing in numbers and strength every day. If Sir Colin gets up here soon, and we are favoured with a fortnight's moderate weather, I believe Lucknow will be ours; but if not, I think we must sit here through the hot weather and rains as in Delhi and lose at least half our men, and *possibly* have to begin again to reconquer India.

I am very much obliged indeed for your kindness and trouble about the pistols, etc., and will accept your rifle with many thanks, and I have no doubt whatever but it will arrive in good time to kill its pandies. The pistols you propose are just what I intended, viz. the Navy or Holster and the small size; the large 5 lb. ones are only used, I believe, in cavalry, and one or two people who got them out by mistake have fitted gun-stocks to them, when they make a light and useful carbine. I did not mention to you one thing about the saddle, forgetting that what every one in India knows, may be new to people at home, viz. that a *very small horse* at home would be a full or rather large one here. I hope I shall get the things safe and soon, and shall have much pleasure in sending you a draft for the outlay.

You ask if I wish to continue in the army. I do most assuredly as long as the row lasts, and thereafter it must depend on what they can give, or feel inclined to give me. At a crisis like the present I consider it a man's duty to do what he can, and not think too much of his reward, but after it is all over I must consider first whether the state of my health will enable me to continue at military duty; 2nd, whether the rank they will give me in the army will, at my age, be worth having; and 3rd, whether I could not, in the new state of things likely to arise in India, provide for my family better otherwise. I fear the answer to all these questions will be against the army, but I shall not give it up without trying my best for a fair position in it.

I am very glad indeed to hear that Helen is better. I hope both you and she may be blessed with health and every happiness, and the children likewise, although my ever seeing them is doubtful.

About the future, one thing seems clear to me, viz. that this country was created to make the fortune of a paper-maker if he could only get the machinery. What would a fair small plant cost to make foolscap and newspaper paper? The newest sort would be no object? labour is so cheap. I think by the time the war is over I might manage the money. – Love to all, and believe me, my dear Bruce, yours sincerely, JOHN CHALMERS

I have not yet had an opportunity to send the sword, matchlock, etc., but hope to have soon.

LETTER XVII

He says: 'I dined with General Outram the day before yesterday.' An ordinary ensign would not normally have dined *tête-à-tête* with so senior a figure as Lieutenant-General Sir James Outram who was now in charge of the forces at the Alum Bagh. Chalmers was not an ordinary ensign, however. He could of course have been sitting close to the general in the mess, with other officers, but a *tête-à-tête* could well have been possible.

LETTER XVIII

Camp before Lucknow,
22nd February 1858.

My dear Mother,

Your letter of the 16th January, with one from Bruce, I received last evening (Sunday), after coming in from a long day's fighting, or at least what is called so here. As usual on Sunday mornings when there is no parade, I was taking an extra sleep. About 7 the commanding officer came and told me to turn out quickly as the enemy were advancing in force in the direction of our camp (the Engineers'), which is more than a mile from Gen. Outram's, and in which the only fighting men are our regiment and two companies of Royal Sappers. Gen. Outram sent us 100 Punjaub Cavalry and 2 light guns to assist us, and out we went to meet them. They, I should say, came our way some 5000 strong – the main body attacking Gen. Outram's camp at the same time. We came within reach of them with the guns about 2 miles from our camp, had a shot or two, when they edged away and tried to get round us, but we were too quick and met them at every turn. This sort of thing lasted until about 3 o'clock, when they got tired of it and went back to the city, but as another attack was expected we were under arms all night. We had only 2 men wounded, as, although at least 7 to 1, the enemy would not come near, and as our business was to protect our camp, we could not go out to them. This is the 3rd or 4th time they have annoyed us this way.

In writing to Bruce, who, I fear, thinks me a sad croaker, I forgot to mention that there was a Captain Campbell of the Engineers at Agra, but that I never met him. He lived in the fort, and as they would not let outsiders in on horseback, except on duty, and I, with some others, struck work and refused to walk, I saw none of the people there except old acquaintances. I may, however, on my return, have an opportunity, when I shall certainly call.

I am very much obliged to Uncle and Aunt Charles for the interest they take in me – also David and the Mortons. Remember me to all of them when you see or write to them.

I wish they would let Harriet Anne go to see you oftener. I have a pair of solid gold bracelets worth, by weight of gold, about £30, for her, and 3 cashmere shawls, *said* to be worth at least £100 altogether. If I get an opportunity I shall send them to you and write to her to go for them. I have been trying to pick up some pearls, and thought I had a splendid set, but found they were paste. I have a very fine Damascus sword and a revolver of native work and very old for

Bruce, and will try to get something of the sort for John Mackenzie before I let Lucknow off. I ordered a set of photograph views of Agra for you and the girls, but the man who does them is very lazy and has not sent them yet. I hope he will, however. I have always regretted that I could not bring down my own instrument. My Cashmere journal and drawings are, I believe, at Goojeranwalla all safe. I wish I had an opportunity of having kept one during this war, but I could not easily have done so.

I am glad to hear from Bruce that Helen is better. Give my love to her and Eliza.

I am glad you like Major Maxwell. I only met him twice or thrice, and he was very civil, but I always rather avoided him.

A son of Doctor Duff's, who is a Doctor, was at our mess lately, and told me a lot of Edinburgh news. He seems to know the Cowans and Merchiston people. – I am, my dear Mother, your aff. son,

JOHN CHALMERS

LETTER XVIII

He refers to 'Uncle and Aunt Charles'. Charles Chalmers was one of his father's younger brothers and the founder of Merchiston Castle School, at which John Chalmers had been a pupil. 'Aunt Charles' was his wife Isabella, and they had several children of whom David (1820–99) was John's first cousin, a year older than himself.

One of his father's sisters, his aunt Jean, had married John Morton, a land agent of Lord Ducie. They had a numerous family.

Harriet Anne was John's young daughter by his first wife Sibyl.

His reference to his camera, Kashmir journal and drawings at Gujranwalla gives the impression that he had occupied his official residence there for a considerable time, during which he had been in charge of a section of the Lahore-Peshawar trunk road. We do not know the length of it for which he was responsible. I remember that, during the colonial period in Nigeria, there were semi-permanent camps of workers at nine-mile intervals along the main roads, to keep them in condition, and a civil engineer would be responsible for much longer stretches.

LETTER XIX

CAMP NEAR LUCKNOW,
28th February 1858.

My dear Bruce,

As Sunday is an Adjutant's comparatively idle day, and as the mutineers seem inclined, for a wonder, to give us a day's rest, and as, moreover, I think from various signs my experience in such matters has led me to notice, that this may be the last day I will have to myself before the assault on Lucknow, I sit down to write you a few lines.

Our force is still almost as small as it was when I last wrote, but I hear Sir Colin is expected to-morrow with considerable re-inforcements. The fascines and gabions we have been making since we came here are now being loaded ready on carts, and packed in proper camel loads. Flying bridges have been constructed for crossing canals and ditches, and the men have been practised in the use of them, and to-day there is a grand consultation between Gen. Napier, the chief Eng., Col. Harnass, the Commander of Royal, and Captn. Taylor, the Commander of Bengal Engineers, and this morning I had instructions to take all the best men off the common guards and put on permanent guards of the old and sickly men, so as to have all the rest ready for immediate work.

My opinion is that to-morrow or next day we will have to try an assault on the town, in which, if we succeed, good and well. We will lose *probably* many men and save a hot weather siege, by which we *must* lose many more.

If we fail in the assault, as we *ought* to do if the numbers against us *fight*, we must, as in Delhi, proceed by regular siege, which will last a short or a long time, according to the distance from the city at which we can get shelter enough to commence. My own impression, however, is that an assault will succeed.

As I have written to my Mother so lately, I shall not again do so until something is settled, as should she know that I was likely to be in another assault within a few days, and any delay should occur in the next letter, she would perhaps be uneasy about it, so I think you may as well not mention the receipt of this; and my only reason for writing it is that, should we assault, as I expect we shall, and should any footing be got (as at Delhi) in the city, I am almost certain to be here, as I was there, obliged to remain with my men to fortify the position so taken, and it might chance here, as it did there, that by so remaining I might lose a post, and consequently you may be an extra fortnight without knowing for certain whether I am hit or not. Now, should any such delay actually occur, you knowing this, can explain it, and you can also say that although I hope and expect to be in the front of my men again as I was in Delhi – (I am glad, by the bye, to hear from my Mother that she saw my name as one of the five who led the first column of assault into the breach there, and which, not having myself seen in the newspapers, I feared was forgotten, and consequently I never mentioned in my letters) – yet the men are now much better disciplined than they were then, and will be much more under control; and as I always wear a beard and dress exactly the same as them, I am no object for a shot at a long distance, as many officers are who wear different colours from their men. Again, I have a sort of presentiment or conviction, or whatever you may call it, that I am not to go under this time – perhaps you may mentally quote the proverb about those who are born to be hanged with the variation of shot for drowned, but at present we keep the hanging pretty much for the other side.

Should anything happen to me, however, I am sure, my dear Bruce, that you will do what you can to console the old lady about it, and tell her it was by far the best thing that could happen to the scamp of the family. Would it also be asking too much of you to kick up a row about my effects, pay, etc., in such a case, as although the amount will be small, it will be useful to my wife and daughter, and also the pension to which they will be entitled, but out of which our liberal Gov. will be sure to try to chisel them on some pretence or other, if no one kicks up a row about it.

I do not know what right I have to trouble one, who is personally a stranger, about such things, and I do not usually do so, but you must blame your own friendly letters and my Mother's constant praise of your kindness for it, and if you object to such trouble, you must so reform your habits as not to induce any one to trespass for the future. Although this letter would perhaps as well not be sent, or might better not have been written, as it might leave an impression on your mind that I have doubts of the work before me, – if so, I cannot blame you, although you would be much mistaken. I never thought of sending a letter before the assault of Delhi, nor should I now, but for you writing that my Mother had been uneasy then; and as for doubt, every one knows that in such a business the chances are rather against than in favour of the few who lead the assault, but I give you every assurance in my power that now I have looked what used to seem like the *certain* approach of death so often in the face as to think nothing whatever of the chance of it, or, if I think at all, it is as a pleasant excitement.

Give my best love to Helen and Eliza and their children for me, also to my Mother; and believe me, my dear Bruce, your sincere friend and brother, JOHN CHALMERS

As I am out of English stamps I must leave you to pay this postage. Some of the friends of officers here have been publishing their letters, and there is a row and threats of courts-martial. It is a shame for any one to do so, as a man writes to his family what is never intended for publication.

LETTER XIX

He mentions typical jobs upon which his men have been employed. Fascines consist of cylindrical faggots of brushwood, bound together and placed beneath the wheels of guns located on soft ground. Gabions are wicker baskets containing earth, used in piles round gun emplacements for purposes similar to those of sandbags, for protection against enemy fire, especially of small arms.

He refers to Brigadier Robert Napier, as he then was, Chief Engineer of the Bengal Army, not to be confused with other members of the Napier family or clan, which included many distinguished military and naval figures, such as General Sir Charles Napier (1782–1853) of Sind. Robert Napier later became Lord Napier of Magdala, GBE, after his successful campaign in Ethiopia. The conquest of Lucknow amounted to a miniature engineers' war in itself. It is of interest that, just before the Mutiny, Napier had been Chalmers's chief in charge of the construction of the whole trunk road from Lahore to Peshawar, so they must have known each other pretty well.

In his penultimate paragraph he tells us that he can now face the prospect of imminent death 'as a pleasant excitement'. Well!

LETTER XX

CAMP DILKOOSHA, NEAR LUCKNOW,
7th March 1858.

My dear Bruce,

A few days ago I wrote to you from Camp Allumbagh (near Lucknow), and said I thought we were likely to have an assault soon, but I have been disappointed. We packed up our traps and, as I expected, we started off, marched some 4 or 5 miles, partly towards and partly round the city, and then after a slight skirmish took this place and sat down in it, and here it seems likely we are to sit. I for one cannot see what Sir Colin is up to, but I suppose he has some plan or other of his own. All I can say is that he seems to be wasting valuable time.

Yesterday Gen. Outram crossed the river Goomtee with his division —5000 infty., 2000 cavy., and 30 guns, and had a fight with the enemy, and I have no doubt the papers will say he won a battle. All I can say from what I saw and know is that with a force far superior to any we ever had in Delhi, he attacked an enclosure and *did not take* it, and that he had a Major of the 2nd D. Gds. killed and *did not* bring away his body. I cannot call this a victory, although the papers, I suppose, may try to do so. To-day Gen. O. again commenced to advance. The enemy came out and met him, and they had a fight. The enemy certainly went back to the city, and Gen. O. as certainly did not go forward. Neither do I call this much of a victory. The honest truth is that as yet we are overmatched, and the odds are rather increasing against us than improving, and must continue to do so with delay. We have now something like 30,000 men of sorts, here and hereabouts, and I feel sure that if Sir Colin would make up his mind, as they did in Delhi at last, and as they should have done months before – to lose a good lot – he will go in and take the place, but every day he sits quietly here the enemy will increase both in numbers and in the strength of their position. Another thing is, that whilst the enemy have the whole produce of the country at their command, we have to draw all our supplies from Delhi and Agra at great expense, and with much labour and difficulty, and now it costs me more to keep my one horse than it did in the Punjaub to keep four. As I have said before, I dare say you think me a croaker, but you have not seen me often wrong since the row broke out.

I think now as I always thought, that to the mutineers we are culpably lenient. Witness the old king and his son, whom the natives say we are afraid to hang, and whose trial has already taken up weeks of valuable time. The evidence that the king ordered the murders is clear, and also that his son witnessed them. To say that the one is too old and the other too young to be responsible for their acts is simply 'rot'. All orders are written entirely in the king's *own hand*, which would not be the case if he were only a tool of others, and his son is 18, and is old enough to have already a family of his own, although I believe not married.

Again, even here in an enemy's country, when every man's hand is against us, who can find a weapon, we are ordered to be careful not to disgust the people by taking their grain and cattle even at a fair value. If they choose to sell to us (which, of course, they do not), good and well, we may buy, but we must pay their price; and if they do not choose to sell we must go without

I myself saw a scoundrel the other day bring a claim against a regiment for £10,000 damages done by their cattle to his crops during the march, and I believe he would have got compensation if I had not been called upon to interpret and threatened to hang him if he did not go off. I saw the damage myself. It certainly was not £10, and the scoundrel had the assurance to ask £10,000, although he and all his village had been in arms against us until we took possession of the district, when, of course, they had either to come in or leave their homes and land vacant, and they knew that they could safely do the former.

This is a beautiful place, and my tent is in an orchard of mango-trees, which give a beautiful shade. The river Goomtee, one of the nicest and clearest I have seen in India, runs within 100 yards of it, and we bathe morning and evening. At first we used to take riflemen with us to keep back the enemy's pickets on the other bank, but since Gen. Outram has crossed we are safe in that direction; the only drawback is that the round-shot from the city sometimes comes in amongst our tents. I have seen 4 or 5 do so in an hour, but as yet they have hurt no one, so we do not trouble ourselves much about them. A round-shot at a long distance is a very harmless sort of thing, as to make it reach, the gun has to be so much elevated that the shot falls nearly straight down and does not roll. A shell in the same circumstances would do a lot of harm, but the pandies have very few of them here, and are saving of them.

This place is a park of the king's, with good houses and gardens all about. It is called Dilkoosha – or delight of the heart. We established our mess in the house next us, which is called Bibi-a- poora, or Gift of the Lady, but Sir Colin, finding out that it was rather a nice place, turned us out and took possession himself, so we are in tents, and find it hot.

Close to this and in the same park is another garden, with summerhouse and statues and all sorts of things. I intend to try to take two of the marble tables back to the Punjaub for a present to a friend of mine, a Lieut. Pollard, who has the most handsome house I know in these parts, and who is one of the most decent fellows, and has a very kind and hospitable wife and four of the prettiest and nicest children I know.

Well, I have pretty well filled my paper with nonsense of one sort or another, and after all have said nothing, but having written that I expected an assault I had to tell you I was disappointed, and that I still am all sound, wind and limb, except my liver, which is sometimes troublesome.

I am glad to see the stir that is making at home against caste and in favour of missions here. I always thought the Gov. policy of discouraging Christians very wrong, but at the same time I thought that for Gov. to constantly declare to the Sepoys that we will not allow your prejudices to be interfered with, and for Gov. servants commanding regiments to preach to their men was wrong, as it tended to make the Sepoys think Gov. was trying to do in an underhand way what it feared to do openly. In my opinion the duty of a Christian Gov. is to afford every protection to men of every religion whatever, and to *exclude* no man from employment *because* he has not been able to think as we do, but at the same time it is, I think, their clear duty to give every fair play to Christians, and where the applicants for employment are otherwise on a par, I think they should certainly select the man whose faith gives the best security for his faithfulness.

Love to my Mother and Helen and the youngsters; and believe me, my dear Bruce, yours very sincerely,   JOHN CHALMERS

LETTER XX

Dilkusha was a large, four-storied mansion, decorated with statues, standing in a fine park, built for the Nawab of Oudh about the year 1800 by the British architect Gore Ouseley, who modelled it on the mansion of Seaton Delaval in Northumberland, designed by the dramatist and architect Sir John Vanbrugh, of the late seventeenth and early eighteenth centuries. It was situated about a mile east south east from the city in 1857, but the whole area, including the mansion, are now within the suburbs.

In this letter Chalmers brings home to us the feelings of an officer in the field trying to explain to himself what the commanders are up to. Such perplexity can be extremely dangerous to the morale of such officers and their men, if too long prolonged, though it can never be wholly avoided. The final assault upon Lucknow took place on 2 March, less than four days later.

Chalmers's vindictive attitude to the old King of Delhi and to mutineers generally was very widespread, and similar to certain modern attitudes to the murderers of the IRA in Ulster today. Responsible governments, when taking account of such vindictiveness, have to consider not only the most effective policies for stamping out mutinies and rebellions, but the long-term effects of their decisions. In the future, stable and, if possible, friendly relationships between communities must be restored and maintained. How long could the British presence in India have been maintained if the old King of Delhi and his son had in fact been hanged as Chalmers envisaged? Indian nationalists may say: 'It only lasted for ninety years.' Others may say: 'It lasted for ninety years.'

His story of the alleged damage done to crops by the cattle of a passing regiment reminds me of a little experience of my own in the Arakan in June 1943. Indian villagers complained that our West African troops had, at night, killed and eaten some of their buffaloes, a charge totally denied by the troops. Since the onset of the monsoon rain had halted our movements for a spell, the general asked me (a junior officer) to hold some kind of inquiry into claims for compensation. A friendly zamindar and landowner allowed me to use the verandah and garden of his house for the purpose. There was a large crowd of spectators, all Muslim and Hindu peasants of the countryside. It was most difficult to discover the truth in such cases. If a complainant was a Hindu, Muslims jeered loudly, assuming that he was a liar throughout. If he was a Muslim (a member of the majority community locally), the crowd would gesticulate and shout in support of him. I decided, whenever it was practicable, to show the crowd that I had my own methods of getting at the truth. I would suspend the proceedings and arrange to be taken in a jeep, with a scribe and a couple of witnesses, to the exact spot at which a buffalo was supposed to have been shot or otherwise killed. If there seemed to be no such place, I would dismiss the case. If there were indeed traces, including those caused by dragging away a large, heavy dead animal, I would arrange for some compensation to be paid. It would have been disastrous to have appeared uncertain about any case. People are as much concerned with certainty as with justice, and, especially in India, will identify the twain.

Chalmers had evidently pondered a great deal before writing his penultimate paragraph about missionaries and the various religions of India. The reader already knows what I think about that.

LETTER XXI

CAMP BEFORE LUCKNOW,
7th March 1858.

My dear Mother,

I have just written Bruce all the news that I can give, but to stick it all into the paper I cramped up my writing so that I hardly think he will manage to read it. As no doubt he will show you the letter, I do not know that anything remains to be said, only I thought you would probably like to have a letter to yourself.

By the bye, there is one thing that I forgot to mention to him, viz. that our regiment is now a regiment of the line and is the 24th Punjaub Infantry. I am rather proud of this, as when they were first enlisted it was so much doubted whether it would be possible to discipline them, that they made them pioneers and not a line regiment, and I take some credit to myself for showing the contrary to be the case.

So well are the authorities pleased with them that they have raised another regiment of the same sort of men.

I am now Adjutant of the 24th Reg. Punjaub Infantry, but I have heard a sort of a whisper that after Lucknow I will, if I continue to be anything, be Lieut. and 2nd in Command, but I am far from sanguine, as I shall never ask for anything, and I have always seen Sir John Lawrence very slow in advancing any one who will not ask loud enough. Indeed, I should not myself be at all surprised if, after the whole thing was over, they found out that it was irregular for me to be adjutant and got rid of me. But if they do, I will let them hear about it, I know.

I hope Helen is quite well by this time. I am myself much better than I could expect. I always am when I have work and excitement. It is afterwards that it tells on me.

This is a beautiful place. I do not wonder at the king wishing to keep it, but he would have done so much better by not kicking up a row, as his people must be beaten in the end, although at present we do not seem to have much to boast of.

Love to Helen and the children, and to John and Eliza when you write; and believe me, my dear Mother, your aff. son,

JOHN CHALMERS

LETTER XXI

Instead of being mere 'irregulars', the little force with whose recruitment, training and discipline in battle he had been continuously associated, was now re-designated as a regular battalion of infantry in the Army of Bengal. He certainly had much to be proud of. As an adjutant (in charge of the administration of personnel) an officer's rank was commonly that of a captain or senior lieutenant, but, despite his hopes of being made a substantive lieutenant, he was held down in the rank of ensign for many weeks to come. Both in the old armies of the Company and in the Indian Army after the Company's abolition, rigid traditions and rules about the ranks of officers, both British and Indian, were maintained. This, I think, has two explanations. First, such rules and traditions correspond with the hierarchical structures both of Indian and of British society, a truly curious historical coincidence. Second, within British society the caste of 'gentlemen' transcended mere insignia of rank, thus permitting, without friction, the perpetuation of rigidity in the rules. The general and the lieutenant, although they exchanged salutes, treated each other as social equals. This, I believe, explains Chalmers's lack of bitterness about his rank. He worried about his pay and his prospective pension, not about his rank.

LETTER XXII

CAMP LUCKNOW,
11th March 1858.

My dear Bruce,

The day before yesterday, after a heavy day's pounding with the guns, a party was paraded to storm the school-house called Le Martinère, about half a mile from the city. As only two companies of our men went, I was not allowed to go with them, but saw the advance from a very short distance indeed.

The force consisted of part of the 42nd, part of the 92nd (Highlanders), the 4th Punjaub Infantry, and two companies of our men, with a reserve of H.M. 53rd and another regiment. They carried Le Martinère almost without opposition, and Major Wyld of the 4th Punj. and our two companies were ordered to occupy a village half-way between it and the city, but on no account to advance further that night. He went on with his men, our two companies and two companies of the 42nd High. who ran away from their regiment after him, and we saw or heard no more of him except his fire (as it was getting dark) until about 8 o'clock, when he sent up to say that he had entered and was holding a part of the city and wanted assistance.

The fact was that when the enemy retired from the village, two companies of his men, our two companies and the two companies of Highlanders, would not be kept back but followed them in.

Altogether it was a very quiet thing and done with little loss. Since then we are advancing slowly and expect to have all the city in 3 or 4 days. We have all our heavy guns in the part we have taken, and are knocking the rest of it about finely.

I was there all day yesterday, but have not been inside to-day. I had my usual luck myself whilst inside the city yesterday, but had a European sergeant, a native officer and 8 Sepoys hit – none killed.

As you may suppose, I am rather put out at not having been with the assault as I expected, but the whole thing was done by one of those lucky accidents that sometimes do happen. Had the enemy got in first and kept us out, it would have taken many days to destroy their fortifications; although only earthwork, they were the strongest I have ever seen. – Love to Mother and Helen, and believe me, yours sincerely, JOHN CHALMERS

LETTER XXII

As in several other letters, Chalmers betrays his lack of feeling for languages, whether Indian or European. He would not otherwise have referred to La Martinière as Le Martinère, and it is not surprising that, after the Mutiny was over, in 1859, when he had lived with Indians for ten years almost without a break, he should have failed a language test, a serious setback for any regimental officer in those days. (See Letter No. XXXI.)

La Martinière, one of the finest buildings of Lucknow, was designed by a remarkable Frenchman, Claude Martin, in the mid-eighteenth century, for his own use. He was the dominant personality among the Europeans of Lucknow. His career was one of extraordinary versatility, for he possessed the talents of a military commander, an engineer, an architect of distinction, and a trader. As a young French officer he had been captured by the British, after which he changed sides and fought with the Company's forces, though he never changed his nationality. Warren Hastings had made him Surveyor of Roads in Bihar, and he became a major-general in 1796. He was one of many Europeans of miscellaneous origins who settled in Lucknow and made money there, whether by service to the Nawabs and their families, or by trading on their own account. They differed greatly from the British and Eurasian community which grew up around the military cantonment of Cawnpore during the same epoch.* La Martinière, named after its designer, had not been completed when he died. It was finished by his Indian assistants, following Martin's plans.

LETTER XXIII

CAMP BEFORE LUCKNOW,
12th March 1858.

My dear Bruce,

I wrote you a few lines the day before yesterday mentioning that we had got a footing in the city and were steadily getting forward. Yesterday I went over to Gen. Outram's camp, who is attacking it from another side, and with whom are two of our companies. He had a goodish fight and took possession of one of the bridges across which the mutineers get their supplies, and got his guns to command the other. He also burned all the straggling houses outside the city on that side, and from which the enemy annoyed our troops. He killed some 500, losing 30 or 40 of his own men.

Yesterday Jung Bahadory came in with 10,000 Ghoorka troops. They are a rum looking little lot, few of them over 5 ft. 2, but are said

---

*Dr Rosie Llewellyn-Jones's book, *A Fatal Friendship*, describes in absorbing detail the story of the Europeans, buildings and parks of Lucknow in the century before the Mutiny. Chalmers recognized the remarkable nature of Lucknow, but probably knew virtually nothing of its history.

to fight well, although their officers are very bad. They will be of use in preventing the escape of mutineers, but I fear not much else.

On my return here from Gen. Outram's camp, I found that we had advanced considerably from this side; indeed, got well into the middle of the city, but we had lost a good many. Captn. Hodson of the irregular cavalry, the best cavalry officer in this, or indeed, I think, any other service, is very dangerously – it is feared mortally – wounded, and what made it worse, he had no business there, as he only went to look on. Major Taylor of the Engineers, whom I first knew as a young lieut. and who has been one of my best friends since, is also wounded, and although not seriously, he has to lie up and is a great loss. As in reality he was the man who planned the taking of Delhi, so he has done everything here and pushed on in the face of the opposition of some very slow coaches we have. The immediate consequence of his wound was the giving up of a quarter of a mile of street we had got, as the Brigadier is said not to have felt himself justified in holding it at the risk of so much loss, without specific orders. Consequently we have to retake it at possibly a heavier loss than at first. I said in my last that Pandy did not fight so well here as in Delhi, and I was so far correct that he would not face us outside and let us get in very softly, but he is standing his ground well now and doing us a lot of harm, far more than he did there after the first day's assault. In fact, but for our six heavy ship guns the sailors brought up (68 pounders), I do not know what we should do, but, of course, they soon shut up the Pandy 18 and 19 pounders.

The sailors are a queer set. Yesterday a lot of Pandies, who were in a house, would *not* be turned out, and were doing a lot of harm by firing from the windows, which were built up with the exception of loop-holes. Three or four sailors objected to this, and took a rather strange way of turning them out. They got up on the roof, made a hole, lit the fuzes of 3 or 4 8-inch shells they carried with them, dropped the shells into the room, and then looked down the hole they had made to see the effect. It was a wonder they escaped themselves, but they have extraordinary luck, and the result of their dodge seemed satisfactory, as the fire from that house was shut up for the day.

It is hard to say when we may have the whole place – not, I think, under a week, if they continue to dispute every foot this way, but they may try to bolt at any moment, although I think they can only escape by some gross mismanagement. We – I mean my regiment – have had 1 sergeant and 1 corporal wounded; 2 native officers wounded, and 2 Sepoys killed and 8 wounded.

Yesterday, when over at Gen. Outram's camp, I went to see the

Badshaie Bagh, or Royal Garden. It is, I believe, mentioned in the *Arabian Nights* as one of the wonders of India, and although I visited it under rather disadvantageous circumstances, viz. a pretty steady shower of every sort of missile, from musket-bullets to 24 lb. shot, I had time to admire it very much.

From what I have seen Oude is by far the best province, and Lucknow by far the finest city, in India.

Our men are bringing out mirrors and pictures from the Begum's (Queen's) Palace that would astonish you, and I have just seen a bed-quilt of gold brocade that must be of great value. One Seikh has a pearl necklace valued £4000. He offered it for sale for £300. I wish I had seen it, but a native banker is the lucky purchaser.

We, of course, cannot plunder, but I hope to pick up a few curiosities by purchase, after everything is quiet, and I must have a horse at any price, as the old animal that carried me here is about done up.

With best love to Mother and Helen, believe me, my dear Bruce, yours sincerely, JOHN CHALMERS

It is hardly fair to inflict letters on you when I have no overland stamps, but I think news from Lucknow direct *must* be of interest at present to every one – far more so than from Delhi, as then the mutiny was on a comparatively small scale.

LETTER XXIII

In his second paragraph he refers incorrectly to Jang Bahadur, a remarkable figure of the epoch. He was actually the Prime Minister, or effective power behind the throne of the kingdom of Nepal, the land of the Gurkhas, whose southern frontier ran along the northern borders of Oudh and Bengal, in the foothills of the Himalayas. During a visit to Britain, impressed by British imperial power, he had decided that the future interest of Nepal must be one of strategic friendship with Britain in India. He persuaded the king to agree and the whole forces of the kingdom were placed at the disposal of the British Governor-General in dealing with the Mutiny. Sir Penderel Moon writes thus:*

The Gurkha force had been furnished by Jang Bahadur, the de facto ruler of Nepal. An able, but unscrupulous man, he had visited

---

**Ibid.*, pp. 741 *et seq.*

England eight years earlier and been so impressed by British power that when the Mutiny broke out, he was confident that the British would triumph in the end and saw in their temporary difficulties a golden opportunity for laying up a store of goodwill. He at once offered military aid, which Canning at first declined. But the disasters of the next few weeks made him change his mind and at the end of July 3,000 Gurkha troops crossed the frontier and operated against mutineers north of Benares, recovering for the British the towns of Gorakhpur, Azamgarh and Jaunpur. Towards the end of the year Jang Bahadur offered more troops and his personal services. This offer was also accepted; and so a Gurka army took part in the final assault on Lucknow.

The reconquest of Lucknow involved several days of the grimmest house-to-house fighting.

Captain William Hodson, as he was during the siege of Delhi, was the commander of the famous troop of cavalrymen known as Hodson's Horse, of mixed British and Indian membership. His personality is described thus by Colonel G. B. Malleson:*

Who was Hodson? Some men are born in advance of their age, others too late for it. Of the latter class was Hodson. Daring, courting danger, reckless and unscrupulous, he was a *condottiere* of the hills, a free lance of the Middle Ages. He joyed in the life of the camps, and revelled in the clang of arms. His music was the call of the trumpet, the battle-field his ball-room. He would have been at home in the camp of Wallenstein at the sack of Magdeburg. In him human suffering awoke no feeling, the shedding of blood caused him no pang, the taking of life brought him no remorse . . .

During the campaign for the recapture of Delhi, Hodson had undertaken, at great personal risk, to get into the city and to capture the old king, Bahadur Shah, and his family and to convey them to the British lines. He did so. On the way back he personally murdered two of the king's sons and a grandson, by shooting them, an appalling act of murder. Malleson gives a most dramatic account of the whole episode.

Chalmers mentions Major Alexander Taylor of the Corps of

Ibid., vol. IV, p. 52 *et seq.*

Engineers. As a captain he had been second in command of the engineers at the siege and recapture of Delhi, and had made himself responsible for the assault plan that was followed. He had decided that the weakest section of the walls of the city would be at their western edge, close to the Jumna river which flowed past the northern wall. His plan was agreed and the breach in the walls made by gunfire, through which Chalmers had led his men in the assault, had been made at the point selected by Taylor.[*]

He refers incorrectly to the Badshah Bagh gardens on the north of the Gumti river, just outside the town, but no doubt describes the looting correctly enough.

LETTER XXIV

LUCKNOW, 20th March 1858.

My dear Bruce,

Last night we fired the last shot at Lucknow, which is now entirely in our hands, and I have just returned from a long ride through the city. Days ago we had the palaces and all the entrenchments, but the Commander-in-Chief is rather a slow old gentleman, and objects to take any place until it is taken for him by some straggling party walking into it by mistake or something of that sort.

The rebel army have walked off with a loss of 3000 men killed and most of their guns taken from them, but they have not gone in a body, and I think are not likely to get together in any great force again. They must feel that they are completely beaten on ground of their own choosing, but we Punjaubees are very much disgusted at their getting away at all, and feel that with the force we had here during the last few days (30,000 or 35,000) they should have been, to use an Americanism, completely chawed up.

I have a short journal of the affair I intend to send you tomorrow or next day, but I am now very busy.

We hope to get back to the Punjaub at once, but our men have such lots of plunder, I do not know how we are to go.

I have a few good pearls and a shawl or two myself, and would have made a fortune if I could only have got a little leisure.

[*] *Ibid.*, vol. IV, p. 5 *et seq.*

I did not know there was such a city in India. I have seen nothing to equal the Kaiser Bagh Palace anywhere.

Love to Mother. Tell her I am still unhurt and will write to her in a day or two, and that I think the row is now over as far as troops are concerned, although there will be lots of work for police. Love to Helen and the children, and believe me, my dear Bruce, yours sincerely, JOHN CHALMERS

LETTER XXIV

The 'slow old gentleman' who was the Commander-in-Chief was, of course, Lieutenant-General Sir Colin Campbell. He was the son of a Glasgow carpenter named Macliver and had adopted the name of Campbell because it sounded a bit more prestigious for one with military aspirations. He was now sixty-six and had been a soldier for half a century, having served with Wellington in Spain as a young man. He had never served in India until his recent arrival after his appointment as Commander-in-Chief. His slowness was associated with great tactical caution, meticulous accuracy, strong personal ambition and a supposedly ferocious temper, a somewhat rare combination of qualities. He later became Field-Marshal Lord Clyde, and died in 1863.

Officers were not supposed to participate in looting.

His sentence 'I did not know there was such a city in India' is interesting. Even in my father's time, in the 1920s and 1930s, most officers, military, civilian, Indian or British, spent their entire careers within the confines of a particular province, which was treated, constitutionally, almost as a separate country. Most of them had very little experience of other provinces. The same can be said about the subcontinent today. John Chalmers thought of himself as a Punjabi and that all India was like the Punjab. The assumption was neither true nor false, which can be said of many other statements about the subcontinent.

Perhaps his short journal will reappear some day.

LETTER XXV

CAMP LUCKNOW,
25th March 1858.

My dear Bruce,

Two or three days ago I wrote to you that we had taken Lucknow, and promised a copy of my journal as soon as I could get time to write it out, but that time has not come yet, as we are employed all day and every day in destroying fortifications and in hunting up parties of Pandies, and we come back too tired to write much.

I will, however, give you a short abstract, and you can see plenty of maps of Lucknow nowadays – at least I see the *Illustrated News* has one which will show you our position.

On the 2nd of March at 1.30 A.M. we left the camp we had occupied for some time between Allumbagh and the fort of Jellalabad, and marched to the Dilkoosha Park which the Commander-in-Chief had taken on the previous day with small loss. We arrived there at about 11, having to halt some hours on the way for orders. We were then encamped between the house called Bibi-a-poora and the river, in a mango orchard which was, however, rather exposed to the enemies' round-shot from a battery at the corner of the La Martinière House next the river.

That evening I went with 30 men to find a ford in the river, and whilst there I was attacked by some of the enemies' skirmishers, but having 6 Lancaster rifles with us, we soon shut them up, although they had one Minie amongst them. A corporal of Royal Sappers knocked over the owner of it, and another took it up. He too went down, and a third also, so they seemed to think it an unsafe article to hold, and went off and left us.

The following two days were occupied in making two bridges of empty casks, which we succeeded in without loss, although under fire, and passed across Gen. Outram with 4000 men to occupy a position opposite the stone and iron bridges, and cut off supplies from that direction.

Up to the 9th we were engaged in preparing materials and putting up batteries to quiet those the enemy had in the Martinière, and on the afternoon of that day the attack was ordered. I saw besides artillery, the 42nd and 93rd Highlanders, the 53rd Queen's and the 4th Punj. Infty. and 200 of our men. There were also some other regiments, the numbers of which I did not notice. I could not get leave to go myself, but was allowed to go part of the distance, viz. to the Dilkoosha House, whence I had a splendid view of the whole affair, and I never saw anything finer than the whole operation. The enemy retreated, but in fair order, and leaving some of their guns behind them. Between the La Martinière and the city to the right is a village, in which was a pretty strong Pandy force, and Major Wyld of the 4th Pun. Inf., with his regiment and 100 of our men, was ordered to clear it. Some 200 Highlanders got off with him, as by this time it was dark, and the next thing that we heard of him was that he was in the city, having followed up and got in with the enemy. The Commander-in-Chief was in a rage at Major W. not obeying orders, but it was too fortunate an affair to say much about, as he had, without loss, got a position inside the first row of fortifications which it would have cost much to take in a regular way.

From this beginning we got steadily on until we got Major Banks's house, and from it went on from house to house and from garden to garden until we got the Begum's house, where 522 of the enemy were killed, and we lost Major Hudson of the Punj. Cav. killed, and my friend Major Taylor of the Engs. wounded.

On the 11th we marched to the La Martinière to have our camp nearer the city, and on the 12th took the Secundra Bagh and the house beyond the Begum's, and got round the end of the second line of fortifications which merely rested on some strong houses, as the Pandies seemed to think we would advance through the open streets and not through the houses as we did. On the 14th we marched close to the city, next to Major Banks's house where our camp now stands, and on the same day, in taking some houses next to the third and last line of entrenchments, a few Seikhs of Major Brazier's regiment again got inside with the enemy and held their ground, and virtually the city was at our command, as they were supported at once, the enemy driven out with considerable slaughter and a loss of upwards of 50 guns. I never saw anything so strong as the earthwork entrenchments, and it is shameful to think how ill so fine a force of Sepoys defended them – at least we think so after Delhi, but some of the Sebastopol people think otherwise and say they never saw heavier fire.

Since that day it has been a steady advance until the date of my last, at which time we had the whole city; but a beast of a Molvie or Mussulman preacher came back with a lot of natives and had a fight on the 22nd, when we lost Capt. Wale of the Punj. Horse killed; Major Wyld, 4th Punj. Infty., severely wounded, and his second in command killed. Major Brazier, Pun. Inf., and his second in command and adjutant, wounded; and Ensign Knowles, of our regiment, wounded. Our Seikhs, that is the 4th and Brazier's and ours, were at first beaten back but rallied and licked the Molvie, taking his 3 guns and a lot of horses, of which I have bought 3 very good ones for £25 – rather a bargain as horses have been going lately, when you could not get anything fit to ride under £100 each. The day before yesterday some of the enemy gathered at a place some 10 miles off, and a force was sent off, when they ran at such a rate that they did not wait for a shot and left 15 guns behind them, but I, for one, think it unfortunate that so many of them have gone off at all, as I fear it has let us into another hot weather campaign – which I should not like.

Our men have lots of plunder, and some that I brought from the Punjaub nine months ago, without a second shirt, are worth hundreds of pounds, I believe. Sir Colin says they are the greatest blackguards in the army, but we can stand the accusation, as our list of killed and wounded bears witness that they fought well for it.

I have myself picked up a few things by purchase from the men, but could not, of course, plunder anything, and if I can get leave home I have some pretty things in the way of valuable arms and a few cashmere shawls, pearls, etc. etc., but the value is not much altogether in that way after all. I have, however, a book that contains the life of the king, in poetry, and has about 100 of the finest native paintings in it I ever saw. I was offered £30 for it yesterday but refused. I had also a book with the photographs of the king and all the family. I gave £10 for it, but Mr. Russell, the *Times* correspondent, persuaded me to give it up to him.

I hope to get an opportunity to send some things home soon.

Give my love to Mother, Helen, and the bairns; and believe me, my dear Bruce, yours sincerely, JOHN CHALMERS

LETTER XXV

Familiarity with Lucknow had improved his spelling.

The name of the Maulvi was Ahmadullah Shah, of Faizabad. He was one of the most effective of the Muslim leaders of the mutineers.

The diary of William Howard Russell, the correspondent of *The Times*, containing an excellent account of the Mutiny, was edited in a shortened version by Michael Edwardes and published by Cassell, London, in 1957, under the title *My Indian Mutiny Diary*.

LETTER XXVI
Camp with General Walpole's Column, near Lucknow, 4th April 1858.

My dear Mother,

Your letter of the 8th Feby. I received two or three days ago, and am very glad to hear that Harriet Anne is to pay you a visit. I wrote a pretty strong letter on the subject the other day, but it could not be received yet, and I am very glad indeed that the visit should be rather the result of a proper feeling on Sibyl's part than an order on mine.

I am very much obliged indeed by Bruce's attention to my wants in the pistol and saddle line. I shall have much pleasure in sending him a draft for the amount as soon as I know what it is, but you do not mention to whom he has sent the pistols in Bombay, and they will not be forwarded to me, I fear, until I have sent money for their carriage.

Our regiment has been divided into two wings for the present. Half of it is to stay here for the summer in garrison, and the other half – Headquarters wing – with which I go, is attached to Gen. Walpole's column, and will have to march about the country to keep it quiet, or perhaps may move to Bareilly to take the city. It is now fearfully hot in tents, and although, as usual, when I have lots to do, I am in excellent health, I really dread another summer under canvas for its probable effects on my constitution, which is rather the worse for wear as it is.

Many thanks for the offers of my friends in my favour. I only wish I knew what they could do, but do not clearly see how they can do anything. I know a statement of my services has gone home with a pretty strong recommendation, but I expect the Gov. will think they do enough if they confirm my Ensigncy and Adjutancy. If so, I shall most certainly not remain with them, as to be an ensign of my age at the *close* of a war, would hold out no prospect of advancement whatever.

If they *confirm* my ensigncy and adjutancy from the time I was appointed, and as a reward for service promote me to Lieut. and second in command, I shall hold on, as in that case I might eventually hope to retire as a Captain, which the other way would hardly be within the range of possibility.

In other respects this affair has done me a great deal of good. I have drawn good pay and allowances, and, in spite of the high prices we have had to pay for everything, have saved money, and I think, nay, I am almost sure, that when I return to the Punjaub I shall be worth £2000 to £2500 at the least, and that is, in this country, an ample capital to commence more than one sort of business on. My hobby has always been, ever since I came to the country, a tea-plantation, and with that capital and moderate industry I think I should do well.

I am now well mounted for the first time since I left the Punjaub, having picked up some good horses here at moderate prices.

With love to Helen and the children, and respects to Bruce, I am, my dear Mother, your aff. son, JOHN

LETTER XXVI

Between this and others of the ensuing letters there are long unexplained gaps, and a few passages are missing. We can only guess at the explanations. Guesswork, however, can perhaps be assisted by a very brief summary of the remaining events before the final defeat of the mutiny. Such events lay principally in two parts of the country, Rohilkhand to the north west of Oudh, and Gwalior to the south of the Jumna river, south east of Agra. Into Rohilkhand had fled many of the mutineers from Delhi and from Lucknow, and an administrative system of sorts had been set up by them at Bareilly, principal city of Rohilkhand, under the rule of Khan Bahadur Khan. He was a leader of the talukdars, landowners of Oudh who had been crudely expropriated by the Company under Dalhousie and by Canning. Brigadier R. Walpole's column had been given the job of pursuing mutineers in the southern reaches of Rohilkhand, roughly between Bareilly and Shajahanpore. The scattered, unpredictable movements of mutineers over Rohilkhand, Oudh, the borders of Nepal and parts of Bihar caused Sir Colin Campbell to break up his army into several columns, led by distinguished soldiers such as Generals Hope Grant, Jones, Coke and others. Brigadier Walpole (later Sir Robert) suffered a severe defeat when he ordered an assault upon a rebel-held fort called Ruiya, a few miles from Bareilly, without adequate reconnaissance. He retrieved his position later by subsequent successes in battles with mutineers. We do not know to what extent John Chalmers was involved in these events.

As for Gwalior, it was in that region that large numbers of mutineers under the Rani of Jhansi and of Tantya Tope had managed to assemble. They were finally crushed in mid-June,

A Sikh sepoy of the 4th Punjab Infantry in 1855, presumably similar in appearance to those of the 24th Regiment, created during the Mutiny and with whom John Chalmers was associated. Painted by Emily Wood after an original engraving by Walter Fane at the National Army Museum.

Delhi 7th September 1875

My Dear John

It seems a very long time since I have written to you, but the fact is I have had nothing to tell you about and my own plans have been so very unsettled that I could hardly say I had any plans at all. Since the Barrack Department was transferred to the Public Works Deptn in 1872, they have been threatning every now and then to get rid of all the old Barrack Masters. They say our pay being according to our army rank is too much for the work we do and that they must get rid of us and get it done cheaper by civilians, or natives, and in this way they have got rid of almost all the Commiss: ried Barrack Masters — by making them feel the uncertainty of their appointments they have driven them to accept any others which offered — or take pensions when they fell due.

Letter written by John Chalmers.

A very few of us whose time to claim pension had not come & who could not easily find any other suitable employment, hung on through thick & thin, backed up by the Commander in Chief who said we had been appointed because a Barrack Masters was an easy appointment and as a reward for former services and that he most decidedly objected to our being turned out —

While all this was going on I of course felt very unsettled as if turned out of this I should have to revert to Regimental Duty, and I knew full well that were this the case, in these days of long range rifles & musketry destruction I would be certain to be brought before a Medical invaliding Committee on account of my sight before I had joined a Corps a week and that the inevitable result must be discharge from the service before I should be entitled to a Captains pension which was not an encouraging prospect — Now however that they have let us hold on so long and that there are so very few of us remaining I am beginning to hope

LEFT *Loyal sepoy, 41st Bengal Native Infantry.* RIGHT *Typical mutineer of one of the Bengal Native Infantry regiments. He retains the scarlet tunic but has discarded the black trousers in favour of the more comfortable Hindu dhoti, and also the white trappings. (Colour plates by G. A. Embleton, published by Osprey Publishing, London.)*

1858, about a month after the virtual defeat of the mutineers in Rohilkhand and Oudh. The rani was killed in battle. Tantya Tope, who had fled, was captured and hanged.

In his letter, when he told his mother that he expected to be marching about the country, he did not yet know whether such movements were to be in Rohilkhand or in Oudh. However, to march about Northern India for the grim purpose of exterminating mutineers between early April and early September was to do so in the worst climatic conditions, first of intense heat and later in drenching rain. In 1858 there were very few roads in Rohilkhand. Marching involved struggling through very rough, thorny country indeed, lacking either water or protection against swarms of insects as soon as the monsoon rain began. Such conditions, especially for a battalion adjutant, were hardly conducive to the composition of letters to relatives in the Scotland of distant memory.

LETTER XXVII

PHILIBEET, 7th Sept. 1858.

My dear Bruce,

Your letter and my Mother's of the 24th July I received here on the 1st. I wrote to my Mother yesterday, and I now write to you that they may go to Bombay by different posts in hopes that one, if not both, may reach safely, as the mails are still sometimes cut off, although not so often as they were 4 or 5 months ago.

I am particularly anxious about these reaching, as I see I am put down in the newspapers by some fool, who would have been better minding his own business, as wounded, and as that may find its way by telegraph, my Mother may be anxious. I for that very reason kept my name out of the official returns, as it was a mere scratch of a sword, that I did not require even to have dressed; thanks to the Colts revolver – the largest – I settled my friend before he became too troublesome. I have not heard of the saddle yet, but no doubt it will come safe, and it was I who was *behind the age*, not you that were wrong in the kind. I find that from your description it is strictly correct according to what the mounted officers of all the regiments *fresh from home* use. I have now two first-rate chargers, but one, a sweet, pretty Arab, is not my own, but as good as mine, as his master can't ride him and uses a steady old horse I used to ride, and gives him to me. He won't sell him, though. He refused £160. The other, a powerful and splendid bay, I plundered at Lucknow. What you say about old acquaintances is true according to English notions, but not here, else how is it that I can't get any *permanent* employment, even an ensigncy? Everything is local, temporary, and officiating, and must remain so until things change. I think Maxwell could scarcely fairly task me with not being on easier terms with him. As far as I recollect, we met at a wedding of a daughter of a friend of his to a friend of mine. He asked me and the person with whom I was on a visit to breakfast next morning. I went, and I don't recollect meeting him since, as I lived some 30 miles away, and went on sick-leave soon after.

I send you a sketch of two fights we have had, viz. on the 29th and 30th of August, and will try to describe them to you, but I do not know anything more difficult than to convey a decent idea of a fight to one who has not seen the ground himself. I also send the extract from the papers – it is a shame for fellows to send such stuff: only 2 officers were wounded out of 7, at least worth mentioning, and the major, Larkins, was *not there at all*. Brigadier Coke of the 1st Punj. Infty, one of the best soldiers in India, says it was the *best* thing of the whole war, and the despatch says, 'The advance of the skirmishers of the 24th P. I., led by Ensign Chalmers, was the admiration of all concerned.' I can assure you I have had lots of congratulations. It is the first time, so far as I know, that a camp, defended by guns in position, has been carried and the guns taken by a force half the strength without guns – neither had we any Europeans. Enough of this, so here goes for description.

About three weeks ago a rebel force established themselves on the hill shown at the bottom of the sketch, called Sirpoorea. They were about 700 infantry, 300 cavy., and had 4 guns, 2 brass 9-pounders, one 4-pounder, and a small iron one. In front they had the lake and morass shown, and in their rear they had a dense forest to retreat to. It reaches for some 20 miles to the foot of the hills.

Their camp was on a sort of double hill with two small clumps of trees, and was very well selected. They began to plunder the country, murder the police, and, in short, play old Harry with everything and everybody.

We did not, of course, like the idea of such a nest of rascals within 14 miles of us, and petitioned the great and gallant General Walpole to let us go at them, but he refused; said they could not be licked without guns and Europeans, that he had neither to spare, and, in short, that he would put the first man that suggested such a thing under arrest.

Well, we changed our ground and got Mr. Lowe the magistrate to request that a party might accompany him as far as

[A sheet of this letter is here missing, which no doubt describes the first day's fighting. The next sheet proceeds as follows:–]

We returned as quick as we could and recommenced work, finishing the entrenchment before night.

In the afternoon Major Sam Browne, 2nd Punj. Cav., joined us with 130 sabres more of his regiment, 170 of the 17th P. I., and 100 Ghooras of the new Kemaon levy, all mere boys. None of the 270 infantry had ever been under fire.

About half-past 10, having done my work, I got to bed, such as it was, in my wet clothes (having brought no change), and about 12 Sam Browne came to my bedside and told me that, having got guides, he intended to attack the camp in the rear about daylight, and for that purpose would march at 2 A.M.; that he had heard such an account of the conduct of my men on the previous day from both Craigie, his second in command, and Lowe the magistrate, that he intended to divide them – 50 for the advance and 50 more for the supports, and to keep the other infantry in reserve.

I, of course, thanked him, and set about my arrangements. As my men had been very tired I did not call them as long as I could help it, but we got away in good time and marched round by the dotted line. When we got out of the wood in rear of the camp and drew up as shown, we found that the enemy were aware of our coming and were drawn up to meet us. They had 4 guns, 300 cavalry, and 700 infantry, according to the accounts of both spies and prisoners. We were 800 yards from them and not a bush lay between to shelter us from their shot.

First came my 50 men in skirmishing order, then 50 yards behind them 50 more of the same as supports; 150 yards behind the supports came the reserve, and we had a troop of cavalry on each flank and a squadron in rear to be ready to pursue the enemy if beaten. We got round-shot from the guns as we fell in, and I told my men not to lose time firing their muskets, but to push on and take the guns at once. Sam Browne asked me if I was ready. 'Yes.' 'Then give your own orders, and don't hurry your men.' 'Shoulder arms! Slope arms!' (that is to carry them sloped over the shoulder, the bayonettes having been previously fixed and the pieces loaded) 'Quick march!' and off we went at a steady pace, 3 miles an hour, and dressed in line as if on parade, in the face of all the shot, grape, and musketry they could give us, without answering a shot. This coolness seemed regularly to confuse them, and they fired badly. When at 30 yards I said 'Double!' (to run), and shouted, and in 20 seconds the guns had changed hands, the gunners were dead or dying, and lots of the infantry the same, but the cavalry were off – off and away towards the wood. Our cavalry to the right suffered severely from a 4-pound gun at E, which, as they advanced, was moved to F, where, with the little iron one, it was taken.

We took 4 guns, 3 elephants, 40 or 50 bullocks, as many horses, and killed at least 300 of the enemy, losing on our part 2 killed and 30 wounded. Poor Browne lost

[The remainder of this letter is also unfortunately missing.]

LETTER XXVII

John Chalmers enclosed a hand-made sketch of the action described in this letter, and I have inserted it after this note, though it is not easy to interpret it.

Pilibhit (wrongly spelt by Chalmers) is a small town thirty-three miles to the north east of Bareilly, and the action described in the letter and the accompanying sketch, in which he excelled himself, must have been one of the last in the final stages of the campaign.

Kaye and Malleson describe the background in Rohilkhand in considerable detail. Whilst too involved for the modern reader to follow closely, it seems right to quote from their account, for Chalmers won a medal for his part in the capture of the guns, and the major role of Captain Sam Browne (later Lieutenant-General Sir Samuel Browne, VC, KCB), is clear.[*]

The force of Pilibhit was commanded by Captain Robert Larkins, 17th. Panjab infantry. It consisted of the 2nd. Panjab cavalry under Captain Sam Browne, the 17th Panjab Infantry, under Captain Larkins, the 24th. Panjab pioneers under Ensign Chalmers, and a detachment of Kumaun levies under Lieutenant Cunliffe. Both Captain Larkins and the chief civil officer, Mr Malcolm Low,

---

[*]Kaye and Malleson, *History of the Indian Mutiny*, Cabinet edition, vol. v, 1889, p. 192 *et seq*. This volume was written by Colonel Malleson. An interesting feature of life among the important British figures in India during the past century is the extent to which they were linked by marriage. Captain Sam Browne, for example, had a sister, Charlotte, who married the future Lieutenant-General Sir George St Patrick Lawrence, one of the elder Lawrence brothers, who also distinguished himself in the Punjab, during and after the Sikh wars.

considered that the occupation of Nuriah by the rebels was at all hazards to be prevented. Larkins accordingly detached a hundred men of the 24th. pioneers and one hundred 2nd. Punjab Cavalry, under Lieutenant Craigie, to hold that village, Mr Low accompanying the party.

Craigie – who was the senior officer, commanded – reached Nuriah on the 28th. of August. On the following morning the rebel chiefs I have named came down with three guns, three hundred infantry, and a hundred cavalry to attack the place. Craigie made excellent dispositions to meet them outside the town, and checked their advance. So well did the rebels fight, however, that, when nineteen of their cavalry met in a hand-to-hand encounter a party of the 2nd Panjab cavalry under Risalder Hakdad Khan, fourteen of the nineteen were killed fighting. This occurred on the left flank. On the right flank Craigie repulsed them in person. Then they fell back on Sirpurah, three miles distant.

Larkins, hearing at Pilibhit the enemy's fire, thought it advisable to reinforce Craigie. Accordingly he directed a hundred and fifty 2nd Panjab cavalry, and a hundred Kumaun levies to proceed at once, under the orders of Captain Sam Browne, to Nuriah at 4 o'clock that evening.

He at once reconnoitred the rebel position. It was on a rising ground or mount, amid the debris of the ruined village of Sirpurah, separated from Nuriah by an inundated tract of country nearly a mile in width, the inundating water varying from one to two feet. From that side Browne saw that it was impossible to attack. It was possible, however, to assail the position from the other side. The energetic magistrate, Mr Malcolm Low, having procured him guides in the persons of an old woman and a boy, Browne started at midnight to make the detour necessary for the success of his plan.

Taking with him two hundred and thirty Panjab cavalry, a hundred and fifty Native Infantry, a hundred 24th pioneers, and a hundred Kumaum levies, Browne worked round the enemy's right flank, and by daybreak reached a position on his left rear admirably adapted for his purpose. The fatigue had been great, and Browne halted for a few minutes to refresh men and horses. Whilst so halting the rebels discovering him, and at once made preparations to resist him, bringing three nine 9-pounders to bear on his advance, and posting one on their proper right flank. There was no time for further rest, so Browne at once moved forward.

Covering his front with skirmishers, and giving them strict orders not to fire, but to use the bayonet only, Browne pushed his infantry forward through some grass jungle which served to screen their movements. Very soon, however, the enemy's guns began to play on his cavalry on the left, which were marching on the open road. Browne, who was with that cavalry, seeing the effect which one of them, fired with grape at eighty yards, was producing, galloped up up to it, accompanied only by an orderly, and at once engaged in a desperate hand-to-hand encounter with the gunners, hoping to prevent them working their piece till the skirmishers should come up. Surrounded by the enemy, who attacked him with great fierceness, Browne attained his object. He did prevent the working of the gun until the skirmishers came up and relieved him. In the fight, however, he was first wounded on the knee; immediately afterwards his left arm was severed at the shoulder. As he received this terrible wound, his horse, struck in the face, reared up and fell back on him. Just then the Wirdi-major of his regiment, followed by two or three others, rushed in, and though the former was severely wounded, they kept the rebels at bay, and saved their commanding officer. Immediately afterwards the infantry came up, bayoneted the gunners and secured the gun which Browne had captured.

To go back for a moment. Whilst Browne was thus engaged the gunners, the skirmishers had advanced steadily without firing a shot until close to the position, when a body of the enemy's infantry lying in the grass jumped up and fired. On this the skirmishers, firing a volley, dashed on, secured the gun, and, aided by the supports and reserve, carried the position.

The cavalry on the right, meanwhile, pushing on, had simultaneously with their comrades on the left, attacked the enemy's flank, and captured one gun. This completed their discomfiture. They broke and fled into the jungle, followed, so far as it was possible to follow them, by the victorious horsemen. Their loss had been heavy, amounting to three hundred men killed, their four guns, their ammunition, and their stores. The two rebel leaders escaped, though one of them, Nizam Ali Khan, had been wounded.

The skirmishers, of course, were Chalmers's men. Browne received his Victoria Cross for this action.

In Kaye and Malleson's account the ranks of some of the officers differ from those attributed to them by Chalmers.

That is probably explained by the rapid subsequent promotions, perhaps in the field.

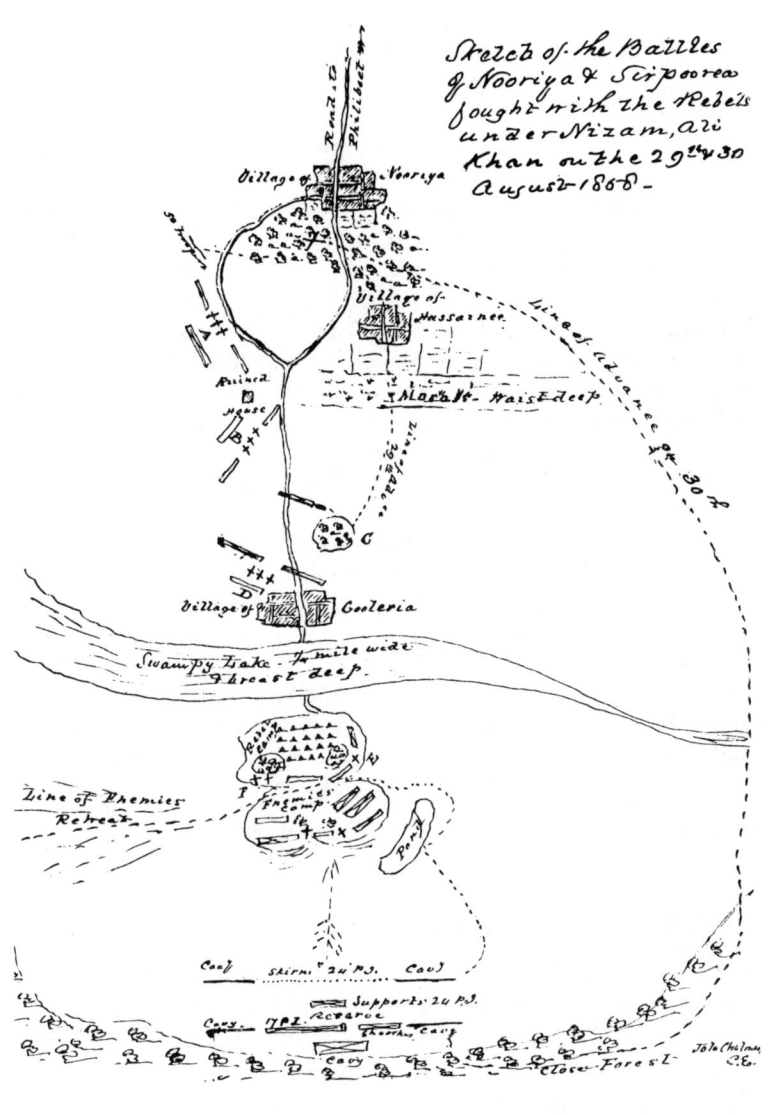

LETTER XXVIII

[The following letter from Colonel John Clarke refers to the same subject as the previous letter.]

JHABPHANPORE, Nov. 29 [1858].

My dear Chalmers,

I hope you have recovered from the wound in the foot, and that your health is generally *fair*, for sound I never can think it will be till you sniff the briny. I am going home sick. I have been very ill, but am now convalescent.

I cannot leave the country without congratulating your p. p. comrades on what I must think one of the most brilliant feats of arms, if not the most so, that has distinguished the Army. It has not been half appreciated (so far as I can see), and for *that* your General and Brig. are responsible. It was not to be supposed that you wounded men could write despatches beyond necessity.

Directly I saw the account (and I saw only a good private one) I wrote to Sir John Lawrence urging your claims to an Unattached Company in H.M.'s service on him, but he took no notice of it. I am going off as soon as Wm. Forbes arrives to relieve me. My dear Chalmers, I wish you luck. Keep your temper, my boy; excuse a *pater*, and I still hope to see you where you ought to be. I wish I had you as a Civil Asst. I don't know if I shall be able to return to India, but I earnestly hope so, for a year or two's work I hope I may have in me. – Yours very truly, J. CLARKE

If you have occasion to write to me, you must address any time before end of Decr., care of Col. H. P. Barm, in Calcutta.

LETTER XXVII

It is gratifying that this letter to Chalmers from an older colleague was found among the others. He would surely have treasured it. The two p's, of course, refer to Chalmers's Punjab Pioneers. From our standpoint the most telling sentence is: 'Keep your temper, my boy . . .' Colonel Clarke must have been aware of Chalmers's tendency to give vent to his feelings among senior colleagues, which, I think, explains the modesty of his rank throughout his service in India.

LETTER XXIX
SHUMSHABAD, NEAR ATTOCK,
12th July 1859.

My dear Mother,
Your letter of the 16th May I received here about a week ago, and I was very glad to hear that you all get on well.

I wrote you some time ago that I had sent you some 15 or 16 wool and silk scarves, and requesting you to distribute them. They reached Elliott safely nearly a month ago, and are now no doubt on the sea. Mrs. Pollard and her little consignment must have reached England ere this. Pollard dined and stopped the night with me last week.

I think I mentioned, when in Umritsar, that on an Easter Tuesday morning I had gone to the baptism of some 6 or 7 native converts. It took place in a small chapel attached to the Church Mission Orphan School, and besides myself, the Judge, his deputy and his assistant, and two or three other influential people attended. Now, as Indian newspapers always interfere with what does not concern them, all our names were published in the next *Lahore Chronicle*. Lord Canning saw it, and immediately wrote to Sir R. Montgomerie, the Lieut.-Governor, to know under what circumstances Government Officers could have done such a thing, and to call upon us for explanation. Sir R. Montgomerie never did so, but I suppose wrote his own sentiments, which shut up the matter for the time.

The other day, however, Lord Canning found out that I was in the habit of reading the Church service in Hindoostanee on Sundays, and that 12 men, 3 women, and 4 children had been baptized, and acted as good and consistent Christians; also that many more attended service and were anxious for baptism; also that I had a school in which 35 men were learning to read and write, and that some of them could read the Scripture fluently.

These men, as I have before written to you, were once all thieves and robbers, and most people would have thought the person who had not only made soldiers of them – and such soldiers as you have seen by my letters they have proved – but also civilised and taught them, deserved some credit. Not so Lord C. He sent a circular to all Punjaub regiments, stating that a strong tendency to embrace the Christian religion had manifested itself in the 24th P. I., and prohibiting all commissioned officers from interfering in this way. I never mentioned this to any one, so I don't know where the *Lahore Chronicle* got the facts, but it gives a very fair statement of all that I did in the matter, so of that I can't complain, but as Lord Canning will be sure to see the article it will ruin my prospects, I fear. Of one thing, however, I am proud, viz. that if I have to leave, I will leave him the *very best regiment* in the service.

You once asked why my men did not petition for me to command. That would be contrary to all rule, and a man who *makes* people work and do their duty, although liked and respected, is not likely to be petitioned for.

Well, when we saw the article in the paper and the order, both Major Hovenden and myself sent in a resignation of our appointments, but Sir Robert Mongomerie refused them, saying that we must wait to see what Lord C. will do next, and that he can't go against the Queen's proclamation.

I hope to start to Cashmere this day month, and to send Bruce some horns and skins. By the bye, Lieut. Stevenson of our corps is in Cashmere now, and has caught the man who robbed me, but has not found the property, although he hopes to do so. – Love to all, and believe me, my dear Mother, your aff. son, JOHN CHALMERS

LETTER XXIX

Attock is in the far North West, just north of Rawalpindi, not far from Peshawar. The Mutiny is now over and Chalmers, with his own troops, is back in the part of the country with which he and his men were most familiar, the troops being at no great distance from their own villages. Presumably they were now to form part of the peacetime garrison of the frontier region.

Major Hovenden and Chalmers had been fellow officers since mid-1857, both having belonged to the original irregular force that had been raised for the long march to the relief of Delhi.

Sir Robert Mongomery (spelt incorrectly by Chalmers) was Lieutenant Governor of the Punjab, appointed in 1851 to succeed Sir John Lawrence. Incidentally, he was the great-uncle of Field-Marshal Lord Montgomery of Alamein). Lord C. of course, was Lord Canning, formerly Governor-General and now Viceroy at Calcutta.

The Royal Proclamation mentioned in the penultimate paragraph had been made on 1 November 1858. It had announced the abolition of the East India Company and the transfer of responsibility for the government of India to the

Crown. It had given various assurances about the future of British policy respecting the independence of the princes and the rights of the various communities. Of widest interest to Indians generally had been the statement in the Proclamation that Her Majesty had no intention to impose the Christian faith upon the people of India, and a promise that none should be 'in any wise favoured, none molested or disquieted, by reason of their religious faith or observance, but that all should alike enjoy the equal and impartial protection of the law'.

Interpreters of the Indian Mutiny will continue to be divided between those who believe that it need not have occurred at all had there been no missionaries, professional or amateur, civil or military, and those who believe that it would not have occurred had there been a lot more of them. My own view is that it was always impossible for more than a tiny minority of Indians to be turned into Christians by *any mere missionaries*, and that perhaps the major cause of the Mutiny was an attempt to achieve the impossible. I refer the reader back to the opening chapter and to the parliamentary debate of 1813.

At the India Office Library I searched in vain for the report in the *Lahore Chronicle* (on microfilm) of the baptismal ceremony at Amritsar to which he refers. He could have had in mind either of two Easter periods and, in any event, the microfilm records are not quite complete. Most of the letters in this collection were written from places to the east of Amritsar. However, in the issue of 27 April 1859 I found a long editorial commencing with an acknowledgement with thanks of a copy of 'the Fourth Report of the Umritsar [*sic*] Branch of the Punjab Mission of the Church Missionary Society from 1st October 1857 to 31st December 1858'. After reporting the baptisms of a few civilian Christians, the article goes on:

One is a servant in the mission ... the other belongs to the 24th. Punjab Infantry, now at Peshawar. For nearly a month, whilst this regiment was at Umritsar, the Gospel was preached to the men daily (by Chalmers himself) and many of them expressed a desire to be further instructed. None, however, were baptised except the one above mentioned. At his baptism many of his comrades were present, and the Rev. Mr Strawbridge was informed that upon his return to the lines, he was received in the most friendly manner.

What a comment is this reception of the converted soldier by his heathen brethren, on the absurd fears which Government, up to very lately, entertained on the subject of conversion in the ranks of the native army. But for the short sighted and faithless policy to which the authorities adhered, and by which a hundred thousand men were compelled to live in bestial error, and of course to bring forth its fruits, the late frightful combination of our soldiery could never have been effected. Had there been but two native Christian sepoys, we will not say in each regiment, but in each cantonment, the machinations of the mutineers must have been dragged to light. It is to be hoped that the eyes of the Government have now been opened, and that there will be henceforth no interference, one way or the other, with the labours of the missionaries among 'all sorts and conditions of men . . .'

Over 130 years have elapsed since the above was written in the hot weather at Lahore. At such retrospect it may seem to modern, less evangelical readers – and certainly to myself – that the head of the editorial ostrich was firmly buried in the evangelical sand of the epoch.

Of what substance did the sand consist? It had two main ingredients. The first was the prevailing notion that the religious faith of a person, whether in India or anywhere else, was just a matter of his or her notions about something called the Truth. Truth was accessible by reasoning and a readiness to surrender the will sufficiently to permit the apprehension of ancient writings, books or lessons, and to participate in particular ritual. The second ingredient was of a negative nature. It amounted to failure to appreciate that in the course of human history the rise to dominance of great religions can be attributed only to a minor extent to the spread of individual, personal, intellectual or moral considerations. They have spread most conspicuously when associated with the dynastic power of rulers whose readiness to put people to death or cause intense physical suffering to them has not been in doubt. Mere missionaries have made converts to their various persuasions only rarely on any large scale. Catholic and Protestant missionaries in parts of the African continent later in the century certainly did so on a considerable scale. Their efforts led to local wars, followed by the establishment of the colonial empires of several European powers. But such instances, together perhaps with the spread of Buddhism during a couple of centuries in the history of ancient India, have been exceptional. The spread of the three great monotheistic religions of Judaism, Islam and Christianity was associated with homicidal savagery, not peaceful 'instruction' of the kind envisaged in the sweaty editorial offices at Lahore, or by members of the House of Commons in 1813. The example of Byzantine Christianity is instructive. For centuries people had their eyes put out, their noses cut off or their tongues hacked out, or were skinned alive or disembowelled, because they were thought to have the wrong ideas about the Holy Ghost, the Trinity, the Virgin or what not. The trouble was not because their ideas were *mistaken*, but because they were the ideas of enemies of the emperor, of adherents to the power of Western Rome, of the Pharaoh of Egypt, or, most fatefully as it turned out, the Prophet. Similarly, the spread of Christianity throughout Europe was associated with burnings at the stake, appalling massacres and bodily horrors of every description. The mutineers of India were acting according to form. The sepoys of the East India Company had no knowledge of the horrors of the European past. But they knew well enough what had been involved in the spread of their own religions in the past. Their heads were well above the sand.

John Chalmers

After the suppression of the Mutiny and the abolition of the East India Company, the armed forces of India were subjected to a long period of financial stringency and structural retrenchment. Whilst the three armies remained in existence, it was the policy of the government to create a single Indian Army with the extremely complex system of distinct regiments, each with its own local and communal traditions, distinctive uniforms and customs, all of which were deeply valued by their possessors. Unification, with the variety preserved, was not achieved until 1895.

Apart from the long-term process of structural unification, problems of establishment had been created during the Mutiny itself by the existence of many officers and units who came into existence fo the purpose of dealing with the Mutiny at speed, but who remained on within the armed forces without beng made redundant. John Chalmers was one of a great many such officers. The establishment problem was dealt with pragmatically by distinguishing between 'regular' officers who 'belonged' to 'regular' regiments of the armies, and those who were described as 'unattached'. John Chalmers, from the date of his first appointment to the newly raised Punjab Pioneers by the Chief Commissioner of the Punjab, Sir John Lawrence, early in 1857, to the day of his death in Devonshire, was always a member of the 'unattached list'.

Unattached officers were available for postings to any job, military or civilian, regular or irregular. They were not deprived either of their entitlement to pensions calculated by length of service or seniority within their changing ranks, or of promotion when vacancies occurred either in regular regiments or in other ways. Many unattached officers were posted for long periods to civilian jobs, such as surveyors and makers of maps, civil engineering, forestry or minerological surveys.

During such spells they were promoted to senior ranks whether or not they had ever commanded forces of the kind normally associated with such ranks. Late in the century, in Britain there were over sixty retired major-generals, mostly from India, few of whom had ever commanded a body of men larger than a battalion or a brigade. Their achievements had usually been of quite different kinds. Some of them, no doubt, had inspired W. S. Gilbert's song about the modern major-general in *The Pirates of Penzance* whose knowledge of matters animal and vegetable made him the very model of a modern major-general. However expensive the system was for the Indian taxpayer, it did somehow smooth the way for the formation of a unified Indian Army of which India has had reason to be proud in war and peace, and contributed something to the colour schemes of garden parties in the southern counties of England.

In September 1859 John Chalmers's own 24th Punjab Pioneers, which had been put together hurriedly at the beginning of the Mutiny, having regard to its excellent services during the war against the mutineers, was redesignated as a regular regiment of the Bengal Army and named the 34th Native Infantry. A little later it was renamed as the 32nd. Chalmers was appointed as a lieutenant of the regiment but, unfortunately for him, only with effect from the date of that appointment, notwithstanding the fact that he had already been promoted to the rank of a lieutenant two and a half years previously. The date of his second appointment would affect both his seniority for promotion purposes, and the level of his eventual pension. Since he was by now thirty-eight years of age and at least ten years older than most other lieutenants, his military prospects were, to say the least, depressing. It worried him greatly, for he did not see how he could ever afford to retire to the humblest sort of cottage in Britain. He petitioned the authorities in vain about his position.

I suspect that he was thus treated for two principal reasons. As to seniority, the authorities wanted to avoid complaints from regular officers that an 'interloper' such as John Chalmers was put ahead of them merely because he was an 'old man' and had done well in the fighting. The second reason, I suspect, was of a personal nature. In bureaucratic hierarchies, whether civil or military, officers are promoted on two main principles. These are (a) personal fitness for the responsibilities of a higher grade or rank and (b) their seniority, based on the dates of their appointments to their existing grades or ranks. I suspect that John Chalmers, however zealous and competent he had shown himself to be, was regarded by his superiors – especially those in distant offices who never met him but made all the decisions far away in Calcutta – as a cantankerous individual who spoke his mind in the mess about anything from the strategy of the high command to the baptism of sepoys at Ambala. He was, moreover, of an age most difficult to fit in easily to the establishment of any regimental mess, where the commanding officer himself would probably be younger than himself. A few grey hairs, in an officers' mess, tend to confer authority not only upon a man's rank, but upon his talk. I do not suppose that the talk of John Chalmers was invariably relished by his superiors during the consumption of their breakfast toast or chapatties. His anxieties, however, must have been acute. Some of them are illustrated in the photographs of a few passages from later letters.

In December 1859 he was put in command of a company of his own regiment, to take part in the first of two expeditions against the Waziri tribesmen, a punitive action because they had murdered a British officer who was travelling in the hills beyond the North West Frontier, but not in Afghanistan. The territory, lying between India and Afghanistan, was not administered by either country. As is clear from later letters, Chalmers had wanted to command the entire battalion on the expedition. All the other companies, however, were kept in the Punjab. He believed, probably rightly, that they were kept back because, as Sikhs, they could be trusted to deal with any trouble which might be caused by Muslims who protested against the expedition directed at other Muslims, the Waziris, beyond the frontier. The expedition was led by Brigadier Sir Neville Chamberlain (later Field-Marshal), one of the outstanding soldiers of the epoch. After the expedition was over,

Chamberlain strongly commended Chalmers and proposed to the Commander-in-Chief in Calcutta that he should be engaged to raise and command a Pioneer Regiment to serve in China during the Second Opium War (1857–60).

Instead of going to China, where the war, in any case, was about to end, Chalmers was given a very different job. With a party of men of the 32nd Infantry, he was employed in excavating a tunnel under the River Indus at Attock, near Peshawar in the far North West. The tunnel would have facilitated the movement of troops or merchandise between the Punjab and the hills beyond the frontier. In his article in *The Merchistonian*, David Chalmers, his cousin, writes as follows:

Among the engineering employments in which Chalmers took part, that of the tunnel under the Indus at Attock in 1862–3 was conspicuous at that time. He took a local charge under the head engineer, and was indefatigable in his exertions in pushing on the remarkable trial operations by running galleries of 1025 feet out of the 1505 required to complete the distance between the shafts sunk on each side of the river. To his great grief, the work was given up, for financial reasons only, but the engineering skill displayed by those in charge was very highly appreciated by all who understood its nature and great engineering difficulties.

From 1863 to 1867 Chalmers was obliged by ill health (he had served continuously in the plains of India for fifteen years) to leave his regiment and was employed as Deputy Conservator of Forests in the Chenab division of the Punjab, in better climatic conditions. His services in this capacity had been requested by Dr Hugh Cleghorn, the Chief Conservator of Forests.

The appointment of Chalmers as a forestry officer for several years is of historical interest, illustrating the elasticity of the whole system of government in India right down to 1947. Over many decades the basic structure had been military. The three armies formed, as it were, an administrative matrix, from which men could always be found, on an *ad hoc* basis, for any task whose expertise was not beyond their personal grasp. Personal fitness was valued more highly than technical proficiency which, however, by some magic, was not in fact conspicuously defective when judged by the results.

In December 1867 John Chalmers was given another opportunity to demonstrate his versatility. He was given the job of raising a body of muleteers for service in the Abyssinian war. He did this by calling together the village headmen of peasants and troops whom he had previously employed on engineering tasks, such as the trunk road and the tunnel. Within fifteen days he managed to enrol, clothe and arm 1,700 men, whom — apart from four who died on the journey — he took, by marches and by sea, to the port of Zulu on the coast of Abyssinia, about forty miles south east of Massawa. There he was ordered to make a road through mountain passes into the interior. Before long, however, the task was abandoned because the war had ended and Magdala had fallen.

At the end of April 1868 he was granted sick leave in Britain after twenty years of continuous service in India. He was suffering partly from a fever contracted in Abyssinia and partly on account of a defect in his eyesight. According to his cousin David Chalmers, he had a warm-hearted reception by his relatives and friends in Scotland, but the article in *The Merchistonian* does not tell us how he lived during his two years in Britain. It seems quite possible that, by then, there had been some reconciliation between Sybil and himself. He does not mention her at all in the letters in this collection until Letter No XXVI dated 4 April 1858, that is nearly ten years after his first arrival in India. He refers to her again in a letter dated 29 November 1859 (not in this collection) in a context which indicates that they were by then in correspondence with each other. It is clear from other letters that he sent many more letters to friends and relatives in Scotland apart from those that were discovered in his mother's house at the close of the century at Wishaw.

We can gather from his own statement of his services (expressed in the third person), that his salary and pensionable emoluments during his spell as Deputy Conservator of Forests were greater than they had been as a lieutenant in the army. He wrote:

At the end of April 1868 he was sent to Europe on medical certificate for the first time in 20 years and was unable to return until October 1870 by reason of constant returns of the fever contracted in Abyssinia, thus losing the valuable staff appointment of Deputy Conservator of Forests in a hill district.

On his return to India he returned to his regiment, now stationed in the cantonment at Lahore. In April 1871 he was promoted to the rank of captain and appointed as barrack master of the cantonment of Delhi, his last job in India before returning to England as a Major in 1880. He became a lieutenant-colonel in England, on his formal retirement in 1883, shortly before his death in the following year.

Let us now stand back from our small acquaintance with John Chalmers and the story told in his letters, and try to see him as a human being whom we might have encountered personally at any time during his life: as a boy at school in Edinburgh, as a very young man determined to marry his Irish girl Sibyl against the wishes of his family, as a bronzed field engineer in charge of a large working party of Sikh soldiers, building a road beneath the blazing sun of the Punjab, smashing his way through the breach in the wall at Delhi, bloodstained sabre in hand, the dead fallen about his feet, leading his Sikhs to the capture of the guns at Pilibhit, reading the gospel to Hindus and Muslims at the little church at Ambala, building his tunnel at Attock, meeting, among the new generation of Europeans at the cantonment in Delhi, the widow Annie Maria Wallace, who was prepared to marry him and go with him on his last leave to England and, finally, as he sat in a deck chair upon the sand at Paignton, listening to the voice of Annie as she read aloud to him a report from India in the columns of *The Times*, because his eyes were so poor.

In the nineteenth century it was almost invariably The Great whose identities were presented in the books of the age. John Chalmers was not among them. In our own world, however, we can see him each week as the hero in a series of stories on our television screens: the tall, strong, sandy-bearded, blue-eyed man of the regiment, able, full of commonsense, eternal stamina, bitter about the Command, warm in love, yet ever ready for the day's march ahead and the sight of death.

Consequences

The volume of 1904, which is considerably shorter than this one, contains a few more of John Chalmers's letters, all of them written in the months after 12 July 1859. I am omitting them because they do not concern the Mutiny, which is a sufficiently compact theme in itself.

It is a characteristic of modern academic historians that they aspire to a personal detachment from overt attempts to identify either causes or consequences, or both, in their documentation of the events of the past. Such detachment is understandable. It resembles the Hindu utterance of the syllable 'om', followed by total silence, to convey the universality of paradox or awareness of the eternally unknown.

At the risk of non-modernity I have already tried to set out some, at least, of the causes of the Mutiny and to attach primacy to one of them. To identify consequences is more problematical. Kaye and Malleson, in their six great volumes, appear to avoid any attempt to single out from all the events which occurred after the Mutiny any that must be specifically attributed to it. The logical fallacy known as *post hoc ergo procter hoc** can be avoided by historians more readily than by physicians. The doctor says to his patient: try these tablets. He cannot make any prescription at all without the ostensible hope that it may perhaps cure the patient's boils. The historian avoids expressing opinions about the consequences of events and can content himself with a mere description of them as they occurred. In this book I aspire to look more like an imitation doctor than an imitation historian.

The causes and consequences of the Mutiny have been

---

*This may be translated as: 'After this, therefore because of it', which, of course, may not be true at all.

viewed very differently by British and Indian writers respectively. And global events in the decades from which they have been seen in retrospect have profoundly affected the standpoints of writers and of everybody else whose opinions have found expression in speech, letters and in the silence of personal reflection. There can never be any escape from the limitations of our own epoch.

It is very evident that the views of people who looked back upon the Mutiny from a period quite close to the events themselves were crucially different from those who did so a century later. A friend has lent to me two enormous volumes, musty with the smell of the past, whose title page reads as follows:

The
HISTORY
of the
INDIAN MUTINY
giving
A detailed account of the Sepoy insurrection in India;
and a concise history of the great military events which
have tended to consolidate British Empire in
Hindostan

BY CHARLES BALL
Illustrated with
BATTLE SCENES, VIEWS OF PLACES, PORTRAITS
AND MAPS
Beautifully engraved on
steel.

VOL I
Printed and published
by
THE LONDON PRINTING AND PUBLISHING COMPANY, LIMITED,
LONDON AND NEW YORK

It carries no date of publication, to ensure its exemption from the impact of time. The two volumes together contain 1,312 pages of closely printed text in double columns and each weighs almost exactly two kilograms. Evidently produced within twenty years of the Mutiny, it is written in a meticulous but compelling style of rolling eloquence. Here are the last few paragraphs of the second volume, on p. 664:

We shall here close the history of the mutinous outbreak of 1857–'58. It is not necessary again to recall to the mental vision of Europe the splendour of the whole panorama of Indian history, from the sailing of the first English merchant ships into the Gulf of Cambay, 1612, and the gorgeous embassy from James I to the great Jehangeer (some three years after), down to the successful development of English civilisation in all its forms of railways, canals, roads, bridges, colleges, and village schools – that have altogether changed the face of the country, and, in the ordinary course of events, will doubtless ultimately change the very natures of its people. There is certainly no need that we should extend these pages merely to remind Englishmen of the transcendent valour exhibited, in the distant fields of Hindostan, by their countrymen, upon all occasions of need, from the days of Clive to those of Colin Campbell; or to tell them of the energy of the Anglo-Indian government, when really roused to action – from its early defiance of the tyrant of Mysore, in 1780, down to the triumphant issue of the late contest, in 1859; since the dignity and ability which characterised the powerful rule of the merchant princes of England over the diademed potentates and swarming millions of their Asiatic empire, has been patent to the world, from the first hour in which the East India Company found work for its hand to do, to the moment when the knell of its departing greatness burst upon the astonished ear of Europe.

The almost unbroken series of brilliant triumphs – by which the hydra of rebellion was crushed, and the mild sceptre of Queen Victoria was extended over a land yet bleeding from the ravages of a cruel and unprovoked war – had, by the Midsummer of 1859, left little little ground for apprehension as to the permanent restoration of tranquillity among the varied races that had become subject to her majesty's direct rule. By valour and energy India had once more been fairly conquered in the field, and it was now that the triumphs of civilisation and of peace were to recommence. The task of reconciling antagonistic races and creeds to the rule of strangers, and of producing order from chaos, and safety from the midst of danger, might be difficult and tardy; but it was not insurmountable; for the *way* was manifest, and the *will* was to it.

We have thus traced the progress of the sepoy revolt of 1857, from its outbreak to its close – following the march of outrage, step by step, to the consummation of the punishment. Remembering that
        'An honest tale speeds best when plainly told;'

it may be that less attention has been paid to ornamentation of style, than to fidelity of detail: and thus, if the work be not so eloquently phrased as some might desire, it nevertheless presents to the world a record of events compiled from authentic sources of information, and as correct, in regard to facts and dates, as careful reference to the irregular and fitful issue of official reports, military despatches, and parliamentary documents, combined with patient investigation, have rendered possible. In the earlier stages of the mutiny, when the mind of Europe was kept in a state of fevered excitement by reports of outrage that reached this country, in the most exaggerated form, much caution was necessary in sifting the *husks* from the *grains* of truth: and it is confidently hoped that the result of the endeavour to record facts only, is such as will entitle these volumes to rank among the standard histories of the era to which they belong.

In 1957, the centenary of the Mutiny, various books appeared in Britain and in India to mark the occasion. One of the best, I think, was by Haraprasad Chattopadhyaya, entitled *The Sepoy Mutiny, 1857; A Social Study and Analysis* (Bookland Private Ltd., Allahabad-Patna). In chapter VIII headed 'Some Consequences of the Mutiny', the author develops interesting interpretations. He says that the suppression of the Mutiny led to a great advance in Westernization and education in English. This, for many years, was accepted by Hindus but rejected by Muslims. The consequence was conducive to the rise of the Hindu middle classes ahead of those of the Muslim community. Formerly it had been the Muslims, using Persian, who had been dominant in the public services. After the Mutiny it was the Hindus who prevailed.

Most Indian writers attribute to the British a deliberate policy of 'divide and rule' in the decades before independence in 1947, and Chattopadhyaya is no exception, but his association of the principle with Westernization, an indirect consequence of the Mutiny, is interesting. In developing his theme he quotes from a despatch by Lord Ellenborough, the Governor-General, in 1843, addressed to Wellington in London: 'I cannot close my eyes to the belief that the race [Muhammedans] is fundamentally hostile to us and our true policy is to reconcile the Hindus.'

Chattopadhyaya emphasizes the association of the expansion of the public services and of the Hindu middle classes with the development of the Indian National Congress in 1885 and the subsequent nationalist movement. The anxieties of the much smaller Muslim middle classes about their future in a Hindu-dominated world led to the demand for a separate state, Pakistan. British policy, in response to the rise of Congress, was a reversion to the older tradition of support for the Muslims. For this, again, they were accused of 'divide and rule' as their main instrument of policy. The question is, when is a policy not a policy? When those responsible for it have no option but to follow it. The policy, advocated strongly by Muslim interests, led to the Indian Councils Act of 1909, which granted separate electorates in the provincial legislatures for Muslim voters, the number of seats reserved for them corresponding roughly with the proportions of Muslims in the various provinces.

Chattopadhyaya is good on the reorganization of the Indian Army:

A radical change came to be introduced in the composition and recruitment of the Indian Native Army. Formerly the sepoys were recruiting mainly from the high caste Hindus of Oudh and the neighbouring areas. This high caste composition of the sepoys and their recruitment from a particular region were adjudged responsible for the undermining of the discipline of the sepoys of the Native Army before the Mutiny. With this bitter experience gained from the Sepoy War the Government of India reorganised the system of the composition and recruitment of the native soldiery after the suppression of the Sepoy Mutiny. Henceforth, as the commissioners suggested, the native Army was to be composed of men of different nationalities, castes and creeds and was to be recruited mainly in the Punjab and not from Oudh. No longer would the native troops be recruited from the Brahmins and Rajputs of Oudh. They came to be replaced by Gurkhas, Pathans and Sikhs of Nepal and the Punjab areas. The high caste Hindus came to be excluded from the Oudh Police Force, which was ordered to be composed of Muslims and Hindu kyasths alone after the suppression of the Mutiny. The Madras Army ceased in course of time to be composed of Telegus and came to be formed of Sikhs, Gurkhas and other martial classes of the north. Thus was the Indian society, civil and military, affected by the Mutiny. To prevent the recurrence of any revolt in the future, the Government of India adopted the policy of creating division and discussion in the civil ranks. The native Army was also purged of dangerous elements, and was ordered to be composed of such martial native races as promised to remain loyal to the government of the future.

The Mutiny, in short, was a precursor to the world of Kipling. J. B. Harrison, of the School of Oriental and African Studies (University of London), wrote an interesting essay, *The Indian Mutiny*, published for the Historical Association by Routledge, Kegan Paul, in 1958, another centenary publication. In paragraphs headed 'The After Effects' he accepts Sir George Otto Trevelyan's assessment in *The Competition Wallah* (*op. cit.*) that the Mutiny engendered a new coldness in British attitudes to India – contrasting

the lively interest in Hindu history, literature and society in the mid-thirties – and the sense of duty done, but no longer a labour of love, found in the writings of the mid-sixties. The Mutiny increased British aloofness, self-conscious rectitude and determination to do good to India, whether appreciated or not. Thus T. G. P. Spear, in an article on the centenary, argued that the Mutiny had accelerated the transformation of India, producing a more rapid expansion of education, of public works, of railway construction. The Indian conservative had been made to realise that he could not put the clock back, the radical that the way forward was through cooperation . . .

It is probably more plausible to see the Mutiny as causing a set back. Military men did not enlarge the scope for Indian talent or reduce that of caste. After strengthening the British element in the army, and putting all artillery in their hands, they increased religious divisions by forming class and caste companies, Muslim, Sikhs and, among the Hindus, Rajput, Jat, Dogra etc. The Princes were preserved as a bulwark, the maintenance of a landed aristocracy in India . . .

Hindu or Muslim reformers had to contend not only with their own, but with British conservatives also.

It is very noticeable that Indian nationalist writers of the 1930s, and later, commonly treated the Mutiny as a sort of failed rehearsal of the kind of revolutionary upheaval to which they aspired in the future. Such thinking, extremely contagious as it was, was inspired by Marxist-Leninist formulae of the epoch and by the advertisement-state of the Soviet Union and its indefatigable Intourist organization. People thus inspired or motivated do not readily adjust their minds to the suggestion that the Mutiny, like the French Revolution, the subsequent revolutions of 1830, 1848, 1870 and 1905, together with the Russian Revolution and, early in the nineteenth century the revolutions in Latin America leading to the overthrow of the Spanish empire, far from promoting the objectives of their homicidal heroes, deferred or indefinitely postponed their achievement. Whether or not the workers of the world have nothing to lose but their chains, as Marx announced, it is not self-evident that any known homicidal procedures have eased or removed any chains at all. And, of course, chains available for the workers come in various styles.

I shall not comment on any of the above interpretations, though it is very tempting to do so, and the task would be rather too easy.

There are two historical considerations with which I shall conclude this essay. First, I believe that the Indian Mutiny was probably the only important event in two or three thousand years of the history of the subcontinent, in which the authority of a dominant class or caste was seriously challenged by forces subordinate to itself. And, even so, the rebellious sepoys and their major leaders, such as the Nana Sahib, the Rani of Jhansi and several others, were none of them members of any lower orders within their own communities. All were, or purported to be, upper-caste figures or their followers. They constituted a rebellious élite, attempting to overthrow another élite, the British power. Most of them were peasants, but they were the upper castes of a rural society. In no sense were they a proletariat, in the Western anachronistic verbiage.

Second, I believe that the history of India has been characterized by a succession of transformations attributable to the initiatives of princely or otherwise dominant powers. When such transformations have included 'reforms' such as Western commentators have in mind, they have not been consequences of rebellions, mutinies, actions (industrial or otherwise), or demands, however menacing, but of the enlightened authority of particular princes or other rulers, including the British. In the Indian durbar, the prince does not make concessions to the demands of anybody. He chooses the sweets and deigns to present them to the hands of those who kneel before his feet. The British had durbars too.

Index

Abyssinia, 142, 178, 179
Afghanistan, 62, 68, 101, 176
Agra, 103, 125, 130, 135, 143
Akbar, 35
Ali, Haider, 16
Ali, Mohammed, 15
Ali, Wajid, 133
Allahabad, 66, 83, 107, 109, 116, 120, 133
Allumbagh (Alumbagh), 132, 134, 137, 142
Amarapoorah, 18
Ambala (Umballa), 50, 103, 117, 179
Anson, Gen, 79, 100, 105
Amritsar (Umritsar), 104, 106, 169, 171
Anderson, Michael, 7
Arakan, 19, 22, 146
Attock, 105, 170, 177, 179

Baba Bhat, 82
Babur, 62
Bagh, Alum, 132, 133, 134, 137, 142, 156
Bagh, Badshah (Badshaie), 152
Bagh, Chajju, 133
Bagh, Kaiser, 155
Bagh, Secundra, 157
Bahadur Shah, 62, 143, 146, 153
Bajee Rao, 73, 80
Ball, Charles, 182
Bareilly, 159, 160, 161
Barnard, Lt-Gen Sir Henry, 102
Barrackpore, 18, 19, 54, 56–7
Bebee Ghur, 84, 85, 128
Belhaven, Lord, 87
Bengal, 18, 19, 20, 22, 38, 54, 55, 93, 119, 152
Bengal Army, 20, 43, 66, 112
Bentinck, Lord William, 17, 18, 41, 73
Berhampore (Barhampur), 55, 56
Bibi-a-poorah, 144, 156
Bihar, 54, 55, 133, 150
Bithoor, 73, 80
Bombay, 13, 15, 40, 105, 108, 129, 131, 135, 159, 161
Brewer, John, 23 (fn)

Brown, Lt-Gen Sir Samuel, VC, 164, 165, 166
Bruce, Henry, 100, 103, 112–61 *passim*
Buddhism, 18, 19, 35, 173
Burma, 18, 19, 55, 68

Calcutta, 13, 15, 16, 18, 28, 37, 40, 42, 50, 58, 74, 106, 109, 118, 119, 122, 125, 129, 130, 131, 133, 170, 176, 177
Campbell, Gen Sir Colin (later Lord Clyde), 70, 130, 131, 133, 135, 136, 140, 143, 144, 154, 155, 160
Canning, Lord, Gov-Gen & Viceroy, 1856–62, 110, 118, 120, 153, 160, 169
Carige, Mr, 86, 87
Carnatic, 15, 36
Cartwright, Col, 20, 21
caste, 20, 37, 45, 49, 52, 78, 86, 105, 145, 186
Cawnpore (Kanpur), 9, 60, 66, 69 (fn), 78–85, 99, 103, 107, 109, 110, 120, 123, 128, 130, 132, 133, 135
Chalmers, Annie Maria, 179
Chalmers, Charles, 10, 87, 138
Chalmers, David, 138, 139, 178
Chalmers, Eliza, 86, 101, 139, 141
Chalmers, Harriet (mother of John), 86, 87, 114, 121, 122, 125, 127, 129, 134, 135, 138, 140, 145, 147, 148, 149, 152, 155, 159, 161, 169
Chalmers, Harriet Anne, 91, 94, 118, 138, 139, 159
Chalmers, Helen, 86, 111, 114, 118, 121, 131, 137, 139, 141, 145, 147, 148, 149, 160
Chalmers, Isabel Grace, 10, 87, 95
Chalmers, John, 9, 11, 15, 33, 50, 58, 65, 86–95, 155, 160, 167, 168, 170, 171, 174–80, 181
Chalmers, Patrick, 10, 86, 87
Chalmers, Sybil, 91, 92, 139, 159, 178, 179
Chalmers, Revd Dr Thomas, DD, 10, 33, 34, 54, 93

Chamberlain, Brig (later Field-Marshal Sir) N.B., 100, 102, 134, 176
Chattopadhyaya, Haraprasad, 184, 185
China, 108, 177
Chittagong, 19, 20
Clarke, Mrs Emma, 83
Cleghorn, Dr Hugh, 177
Clydesdale Distillery, 87, 92
Condé, Maj-Gen Prince of, 95
Cornwallis, Lord, Gov-Gen 1786–93 & 1805, 28, 36
Cowan family, 95, 139
Craigie, Col, 165

Dalhousie, Lord, Gov-Gen 1846–56, 69, 74, 160
Damodar, adopted son of Rani of Jhansi, 73, 76
Delhi, 7, 50, 59; massacre & recapture, 61–5; 74, 79; 100–79 *passim*
Dilkoosha (Dilkusha), park near Lucknow, 142, 144, 145, 156
Dinapore, 55
Dondo Pant (Nana Sahib), *see* Nana Sahib
Douglas, Capt, 63
Dunlop, Capt, 74, 75

East India Company (British), 13, 14, 15, 23, 24, 28, 40, 43, 62, 170, 174
East Indian Company (French), 13, 14
Edwardes, Michael, 158
Ellenborough, Lord, Gov-Gen 1843, 184

Falcon, Capt R. W., 116
Ferozepore (Ferozepur), 100, 101, 103, 104
Fraser, Jane (later Grant), 28
Futtygurh (Feteghur), 103, 106, 128, 130

Gangadhar Rao, 73
Ganges, River, 30, 43, 55, 66, 78, 84
Ghoorka (Gurkha), 150, 152
Gibraltar, 93, 131
Gillespie, Col, 16
Glenelg, Lord, 28, 32, 40, 53
Goojeranwala (Gujranwala), 94, 104, 107, 110, 116, 119, 139
Grace, Pratt (later Mrs Thomas Chalmers), 10
Grant, Brig Charles, Barrackpore, 58
Grant, Charles, senior, MP, 28, 36

Gumti (Goomtee) river, 66, 143, 144, 154
Gwalior, 72, 78, 160

Hansi, 103
Hardinge, Viscount, Gov-Gen 1844–7, 67
Harrison, J. B., 186
Hastings, Warren, 25, 40, 150
Havelock, Gen Sir Henry, 60, 70
Hearsey, Maj-Gen, 57, 58
Hibbert, Christopher, 8, 82 (fn)
Hinduism, Hindus, 29, 30, 35, 37, 45, 66, 80, 184
Hodson, Capt William, 151
Hpo-Dau-Hpayah, 18
Hughes, Nathaniel, 92 (and fn), 100, 103
Hughes, Sybil, 94
Hutchinson, Capt, 93
Hyderabad, Nizam of, 16, 17

Indus, River, 43, 119, 177
Irrawaddy, River, 18
irrigation, 24, 43, 119

Jellalabad, 156
Jhansi, 72–7, 99, 109, 123
Jhansi, Maharajas of, 73, 74
Jhansi, Rani of, 73–5, 160, 187
Jones, Dr Llewellyn, 67 (fn), 150
Jullunder, 104, 112, 113
Jumna river, 62, 122
Jung Bhadory (Jang Bahadur of Nepal), 150

Karnal (Kurnaul), 102, 103, 117
Kaye, Sir John, 56 (fn), 62, 122, 133 (fn), 164 (and fn), 181
Khan, Bahadur, 160
Khan, Risaldar Hakdad, 165
Kshatryas, warrior and princely caste, 66
Kumaon Levies, 165

Lahore, 100, 104, 106, 123, 124, 131, 173, 179
Lahore Chronicle, The, 115, 116, 169, 171, 172
Lahore-Peshawar road, 94
Larkins, Capt Robert, 162, 164, 165
Lawrence, Sir Henry, Bt, Chief Commissioner Oudh, 69
Lawrence, Sir John, Chief Commissioner and Lt-Gen Punjab, later Viceroy, 69, 108, 110, 111, 112, 115, 118, 120, 131, 134, 147, 168

Lawrence, Sir John, Bt, 69 (fn)
Lockhart, Graham, 134
Loodiana (Ludianah), 103, 106, 112, 114, 115, 117
Lucknow, 7, 9, 66–71, 99, 106, 109, 123, 128–62 *passim*

Macaulay, Lord, 41
Mackenzie, John Munro (brother-in-law), 90, 101, 129
Mackenzie, John Hugo Munro, 'Jock', 7, 8, 9, 11, 95
Macleod, Col, 95
Mackintosh, Sir James, 37
Macliver, 155
Madras, 13, 15, 17, 20, 105, 108
Magdala, Ethiopia, 178
Mahrattas, 14, 78
Malleson, Col, 56 (fn), 75–6, 122, 132, 133 (fn), 153, 164 (and fn), 166, 181
Manghal Pande, 58
Manila, 20
Martin, Claude, 150
Martinière, La, 76, 148, 149, 150, 156, 157
Mason, Philip, 20
Massawa, 178
Maulvi (Molvi), The, Ahmadullah Shah of Faizabad, 157, 158
Maxwell, Maj, 134, 139, 162
Meerut (Merutt), 59, 60, 61, 62, 63, 74, 79, 100, 103
Merchiston Castle School, Edinburgh, 7, 10, 87, 139
Merchistonian, The, 7, 177
missionaries, 27, 33, 40, 42, 45, 46, 145, 147, 171, 172
Moghul Empire, 14, 62, 63, 66, 72, 78
Montgomery, Sir Robert, 119, 169, 170
Moon, Sir Penderel, 68, 69, 152
Morton family, 138, 139
Multan (Mooltan), 104, 106
Murdan, 100, 101
musket, 50, 58, 79
Mutiny, Indian, 9, 10, 11, 15, 40, 48, 50–85, 132, 158, 160, 170, 171, 181
Muzbees (Mahzhbis), 115
Mysore, 15, 16, 18

Nana Sahib (Dondo Pant), 73, 80, 187
Napier, Gen Sir Charles, 142
Napier, Brig, later Lord N. of Magdala, 140, 142
Napoleon, Louis, III, Emperor of the French, 131 (and fn), 132

Napoleonic Wars, 13, 21, 23, 87
Naushera, 101, 105
Neill, Brig James, 60, 70, 85
Nicholson, Col, 106, 108, 110, 112, 113, 125, 126, 128, 134
Nigeria, 139
Norgate, Col J. T., 46
Northumberland (troopship), 93, 94
North-West Frontier, 120, 176
Nuriah, 165

opium, 39, 40, 177
Oudh, 46, 66, 78, 101, 103, 133, 145, 152, 160, 161
Outram, Lt-Gen Sir James, 136, 137, 138, 143, 150, 151, 156

Paget, Gen Sir Edward, 21, 22
Paignton, 112, 179
Palmerston, Viscount, 131, 132
Pande, Sita Ram, 46, 47
Patna, 45, 55, 133
Phagy-Dau, ruler at Ava, Burma, 18
Pioneers, 110, 174, 175
Peshawar (Peshawur), 100, 101, 105, 170
Peshwa, of Poona, 72, 73
Philour (Philur), 103, 104, 106, 112, 113, 114
Pilibhit (Philibhit), 161, 165, 179
Pitt (the younger), William, 14
Pollard, Lieut, 144, 169
Portsmouth, 95
Pratt, Grace, 10
Princes, Indian, 13, 68, 110, 171, 186
Punjab, 16, 78, 91, 94, 100, 103, 105, 106, 107, 119, 125, 131, 143, 154, 155, 158, 159, 160, 169, 176, 177, 179
Punjab Cavalry, 138, 157, 165
Punjab Frontier Force, 103
Punjab Infantry, 147, 149, 156, 162, 165, 171
Punjab Military Police, 103, 123

Rajpoora, 115, 117
Ramchandra Rao, Jhansi, 73
Ravee (Ravi), River, 104
Rawalpindi, 104, 170
Red Fort, Delhi, 122
Ricketts, Mr, 113, 114
Rohilcund (Rohilcand), 107, 160, 161
Roorkee, 94
Rose, Maj-Gen Sir Hugh, 77
Ruiya, fort, 160

Russell, W. H., *Times* correspondent, 158

Sappers and Miners, Royal Corps of, 93
Sappers and Miners, Bengal Army, 123, 124
Sealkot (Sialkot), 50, 104, 116
Seetapore (Sitapore), 103, 106
Singh, Govind, 116
Sirpooriah (Sirpurah), 162, 165
Skene, Capt Alexander, Jhansi, 74, 75
Sleeman, Sir William, Lucknow, 67, 68, 69 (fn)
Smith, Maj Baird, Delhi, 123, 124
Sutledge (Sutlej), river, 103
Spain, 20, 155
Spottiswoode, Col, 100, 101, 186
Strawbridge, Revd, 172
suttee, 18, 37–9, 41

Tahmankar, D. V., 72 (fn)
Talukhdars (Talookdars), of Rani of Jhansi, 67, 160
Tangier, 95
Taylor, Capt Alexander, 140, 151, 153–4, 157
Thomason College of Civil Engineering, Roorkee, 93, 94

thugs, 18, 115
Tippoo Sahib, 16, 17
Topo, Tantya, 160, 161
Toulon, 131
Trevelyan, Sir George Otto, 120, 186

Vanbrugh, John, 145
Vellore, mutiny at (1806), 15, 16, 17

Walpole, Brig Sir Robert, 159, 163
Waziri campaigns, 99
Waziri tribesmen, 11, 176
Wellesley, Arthur, later Duke of Wellington, 16, 21, 23, 155, 184
Wheeler, Maj-Gen Sir Hugh, Cawnpore, 79, 80, 81, 82, 83, 109, 129, 130
Wheeler, Ulrica, 83
Wilberforce, William, 25, 33, 54
Wilson, Brig Archdale, 123, 124
Windham (Wyndham), Maj-Gen C. A., 130, 133
Wishaw, 9, 87, 90, 103, 129, 178

Yalland, Mrs Zoë, 78, 84 (fn)

Zulu, Abyssinia, 178